ENDORSEMENTS

"*Deep Calling* is the best book on discipleship I've read. Tara VinCross's fresh, engaging pictures of Jesus and church and life—in tandem with her refreshing authenticity over the everyday glory (and struggle) of following Him and helping others do the same—is what our 'post-pandemic' lives are needing!"

— **DWIGHT NELSON, DMIN,** Lead Pastor, Pioneer Memorial Church Author of *The Chosen*, *Pursuing the Passion of Jesus*, and other titles

"A wise woman (Tara VinCross) once said, 'Reading a menu is fundamentally different than tasting a meal.' I've become convinced that is what we often do in church. I am so excited that this book is a cookbook of sorts. It cuts through the complexity of concepts related to discipleship and presents a recipe for an amazing discipleship journey. This is the book I didn't know I needed, both personally and professionally."

— **ANDREA TRUSTY KING, PHD,** Senior Pastor, 16th Street Seventh-day Adventist Church; Author of *Queen in Me* and *Finding Christ*

"In a genre that can too often fixate on individual piety, VinCross manages to keep readers focused outward, on discipleship as a call to our communities. She does not pretend this is an easy task. But she is convinced it is the call of Jesus in and to our world today. VinCross clearly experiences a close relationship with her God and believes in her bones that nothing is more important than being a disciple and making disciples. This, she believes, is sacred work. As one privileged to know the author, I know that she authentically lives the ideas and values she shares."

— **KENDRA HALOVIAK VALENTINE, PHD,** Associate Professor, La Sierra University; Author of *Worlds at War*, *Nations in Song* and *Signs to Life*

"Finally, a discipleship book that engages the head and the heart. Tara skillfully defines the essence of discipleship while simultaneously calling us into deeper levels of discipleship. If you are seeking to go deeper in your Christian experience, this book is a must read."

— **MYRON EDMONDS, DMIN,** Lead Pastor of Grace Community; Author of *The Frustrated Leader* and *40 Days to Life-Changing Family Worship*

"At a time when most Christians confuse involvement with discipleship, this book gives absolute clarity to the true making and growing of disciples. Anyone passionate about connecting with and fulfilling their own life purpose should go on this book's journey. It will not only change the world around, it will change your world."

— **ROY ICE,** Speaker/Director of Faith For Today
Author of *The 12 People You Love*

"In this very practical book, *Deep Calling: on being and growing disciples*, Pastor Tara VinCross very thoughtfully challenges, edifies, and helps to equip spiritual leaders to truly follow Jesus Christ and lead others in the process of doing the same. I have not yet encountered such a relevant, practically useful, spiritually deep and theologically sound resource. This is not a one-time read. It is a book I am anxious to read again and again. This book is a must for every pastor's library."

— **TRICIA WYNN PAYNE, MDIV,** Senior Pastor, Conant Gardens Seventh-day Adventist Church; Author of *The Fight for My Life*

"A refreshing and thought-provoking new perspective on discipleship. Tara VinCross has reminded us of the biblical mandate of discipleship — to equip and develop disciples as change agents of their communities for the Kingdom of God."

— **SUNG KWON, PHD, DMIN,** Executive Director, North American Division Adventist Community Services
Author of *Burst the Bubble: Finding Your Passion for Community Outreach*

"In this book, Pastor VinCross cuts to the heart of what it means to be a disciple. Rich pastoral and personal experience, combined with clear theological insights, makes this an invaluable guide to following Jesus. At a time of high apostasy rates, this is a practical 'how-to' that the church desperately needs."

— **GARY KRAUSE, PHD,** Director of Adventist Mission, General Conference
Author of *God's Great Missionaries*

DEEP CALLING

on being & growing disciples

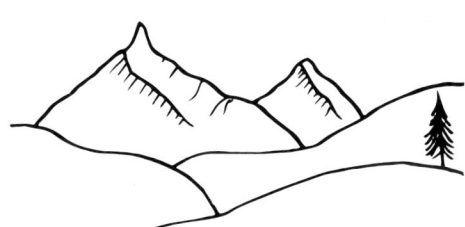

Tara J. VinCross

Forward by Daniel R. Jackson

Copyright © 2020 Tara J. VinCross
All rights reserved. No part of this book may be reproduced, distributed or transmitted in any form by any means, graphic, electronic, or mechanical, without permission from the author, except in the case of reviews, quotes, or references.

Cover and interior illustrations: Amber Haney, ahaneyart.com
Layout and graphic design: Rachel Ortiz, rortizdesign.com
Author photo: Summer Medina, summermedina.com
Edited by Jason Vanderlaan, balmandblade.com

AdventSource

Published by AdventSource
www.adventsource.org

All Scripture quotations, unless otherwise indicated, are taken from the New International Version. Copyright 1973, 1978, 1984, 2011 by Biblica.

Library of Congress Control Number: 2020942776
ISBN: 978-1-62909-761-9

Printed in the United States of America

DEDICATION

For Caleb

To my beloved, your unfailing love, your quirky sense of humor, and your deep awareness of the sacred have changed my life for the better. I love you with all my heart.

For Our Children

Josiah Edward and Ava Sofia, God loves you deeply and so do I. One of the greatest gifts of my life is being your mama. May you awaken to the wonder and mystery of God.

For God

To my God, You are my life and my love. In you I live and move and have my being. May this offering of word and testimony bring you glory and delight.

> *"Deep calls to deep… all your waves and breakers have swept over me."*
> PSALM 42:7

ACKNOWLEDGEMENTS

This work is a culmination of mentoring and nurture received, and lessons learned from childhood until now, making it impossible to name every person to which I want to express gratitude. Still, I want to express special thanks…

…To Brad Forbes and his team at AdventSource for believing in the importance of discipleship in the local church!

…To Amber Haney for her cover art and the artwork throughout this book that brings it to life.
…To Rachel Ortiz for beautiful typography, layout, and design, as well as her friendship.
…To Jason Vanderlaan who served as editor, offered encouragement, attention to detail, and personal investment in this project.

…To Pastor Cindy Tutsch who created a safe space for the Holy Spirit to grow me in Jesus and who remains a dear mentor and friend to this day.

…To Alan Walshe, Doctor of Ministry cohort director and professor for inspiration, perspective, and unwavering modeling of what the life of discipleship and disciple-making looks like.

…To A. Allan Martin mentor, professor, and friend, for your listening ear, unshakable hope, and consistent ministry of presence.

…To S. Joseph Kidder advisor and professor for heartfelt prayers, interest in my growth, and living a life that shows the importance of discipleship.

…To the communities of faith that have journeyed with me in the past. Auburn Academy, Renton, Chestnut Hill, and REACH Philadelphia, my life is better because of you. You made space for me to grow personally and professionally. With heartfelt gratitude.

…To Azure Hills Church. Thank you for embracing me as your pastor and for living the reality of the incarnation. You are God's love in the flesh and it's breathtakingly beautiful to experience!

…To our pastoral team, Mike and Starla Leno, Jessie Lopez, Samantha Peralta, Trevan Osborn, Bryant Taylor, and Nick Snell, plus Nanette Pittenger and Janet Bottroff, who are partners in ministry through the highs and lows and who offer enthusiasm and prayer, humor and presence through it all. I am so grateful for you.

…To administrators who have supported and nurtured space for discipleship, Dave Weigley, Frank Bonderant, Ray Hartwell, Barry Tryon, Glenn and his late wife Barbara Aufderhar, Ron Wisbey, Rob Vandeman, Sandra Roberts, and the late Lenard Jaecks.

…To my pastoral colleagues and friends over the years, specifically Tiffany Brown, Angel Smith, Jason Vanderlaan, William Bonilla, Damian Chandler, Chris Oberg, Tim Madding, Nick and Deanne Snell, and Jim Wibberding for offering encouragement and suggestions when this project was still in its infancy, and for the shared life that made this possible.

…To those who have been through the discipleship journey, which now bears the name Deep Calling. Thank you for stepping out, showing up, and for sharing who you are. Thank you for allowing me the privilege of accompanying you on your journey.

…To Kendra Haloviak Valentine, a sister, colleague, and friend, for your depth, transparency, and humor. I treasure you.

…To my Salt Sisters - Emily, Raewyn, and Rochelle. Thank you for your courage, vulnerability, and grace. The gift of you friendship and the rhythm of our life together has profoundly impacted who I am today. You are my soul sisters.

…To my mother, Camey Jenson for her belief in me and her own example of determination and seeking. To my late father, Edward Vinyard for cheering me on in my calling. To my late mother-in-law Dorothy for her prayers and her delight in Jesus.

…To my children, Josiah Edward and Ava Sofia. May you embrace the wonder, the beauty, and the mystery of God. God loves you deeply and so do I.

…To the one I love - my partner Caleb. Thank you for your support that made this journey, and this book, possible. I love life with you. You make me more fully alive, and I hope each day to do the same for you. Thank you for always believing in me. I love you.

CONTENTS

FORWARD 11
PREFACE 13

Part 1: The Discipleship Journey

CHAPTER 0 Making Space for God 16
CHAPTER 1 You Will Be Like a Tree 30
CHAPTER 2 What is Discipleship? 36
CHAPTER 3 The Experience of Discipleship 45
CHAPTER 4 All Are Invited 54
CHAPTER 5 Bringing the Pieces Together 64
CHAPTER 6 What's Bothering You? 75
CHAPTER 7 Discipleship and the Adventist Church 83

Part 2: The Call of God

CHAPTER 8 Foundational Values of Discipleship 95
CHAPTER 9 Eight Calls to a Deeper Life 106

God: Cultivate Spiritual Growth

CHAPTER 10 A Call to Devotion: Daily Rhythm of Love 115
CHAPTER 11 A Call to Prayer: Conversation with God 125
CHAPTER 12 A Call to Rest: Sabbath Restoration 137

Community: Nurture Relationships

| CHAPTER 13 | **A Call to Community: Life Together** | 147 |
| CHAPTER 14 | **A Call to Healing: Wholeness in Brokenness** | 157 |

Purpose: Develop Service

CHAPTER 15	**A Call to Witness: Tell Your Story**	168
CHAPTER 16	**A Call to Serve: Incarnation**	178
CHAPTER 17	**A Call to Bless: The Prophetic Voice**	187

Part 3: The Discipleship Movement

CHAPTER 18	**How Do We Change Anyway?**	196
CHAPTER 19	**Process, Not Destination**	205
CHAPTER 20	**Where Do You Go From Here?**	214
CHAPTER 21	**And Then, Everything Changed…**	223

EPILOGUE		231
ENDNOTES		233
APPENDIX		245

FORWARD

Tara VinCross takes us to the very core of God's missionary enterprise in this book. While filled with practical illustrations, the book emulates Stephen Covey's stated ideal, "the main thing is to keep the main thing the main thing."

Essential to the ministry and message of Jesus Christ was the call to discipleship. Many conclude that the invitation of God into a relationship is a call to give assent to a given theology, to let it sink in and then preach it to a world that needs to hear it. While partially true, at the root of Jesus' invitation there is a call to the cross. He tells us that, "If any man (person) would come after me He must take up His cross and follow me" (Luke 9:23).

His words have a far-reaching element to them. They move from the superficial and perfunctory and into the most intimate corners of a relationship. No one should deny that, for a Christian, mental assent to a theological framework, and understanding it, are important in the act of "following" Jesus. However, it primarily means that we will give our lives to Him in devotion and service; that in following Him we will be sharing Him in terms of how we live, how we work, how we play, and how we worship. Our connection with Him makes us disciples.

Many years ago now I was walking along a side walk when I came upon a little lad sitting in the middle of the walk. With all of the exuberance of a child he looked at me and announced: "I've got a worm!" He had found it there after a rainstorm and he was intentionally announcing to anyone who would listen what it was that he possessed.

God calls upon us to be intentional when it comes to announcing to the world what it is exactly that we have. Discipleship is the natural outgrowth of a relationship. "Look what I have!"

ought to be the cry of Christianity. God has given Himself to all humanity for the express purpose of building eternal relationships. Certainly, if a little boy could be proud of the worm that he had in his possession, what is it that we should be proclaiming to the world about what we have received?

Finally, the call of God to the individual is a call to inspired intentionality. As it was for Jeremiah, our realization of the precious gift is like a "fire in our bones" that will not allow us to remain silent. For the disciple of Jesus the matter becomes one of intentionality. We seek opportunities to serve in everything we do. Our lives become living testimonies to His grace. Our work becomes far more than a financial means to and end, but rather that which facilitates our testimony for Him. Our proclamation is not just a "clanging cymbal," but a vital expression of all that God has done, is doing, and will do for us in Jesus Christ.

A practical book on discipleship! Praise God! What a tremendous blessing to the church preparing for the final thrust of God's great evangelistic enterprise on planet Earth.

DANIEL R. JACKSON
President (Retired), North American Division of Seventh-day Adventists

PREFACE

Great is Thy faithfulness!
Great is Thy faithfulness!
Morning by morning new mercies I see.
All I have needed Thy hand hath provided;
Great is Thy faithfulness, Lord, unto me!

I can sing *Great is Thy Faithfulness* with my whole heart and from my experience. I have found God's faithfulness to be true in my life.

> Through the pain of childhood –
> dysfunction, divorce, and distress.
>
> Through sexism and discrimination.
>
> Through anxiety attacks.
>
> Through miscarriages.
>
> Through disappointment layered on loss.
>
> Through near-death experiences.
>
> Through caring for and losing two parents to cancer.
>
> Through adopting two times, one on each coast.
>
> Great is your faithfulness.

Theology is autobiography.

My understanding of God has come as I have lived this life journey. These things I have experienced, and the presence of God, in the midst of those experiences, has changed me. Here I am. Alive, whole, and healing. God's deep call to me has ushered me into a place that I would not be on my own. God has anointed me and renewed my call. We don't control what happens to us, but many times we can choose how we open ourselves to growth. Then, for the times we cannot choose, it is simply grace upon grace.

"I became a servant of this gospel by the gift of God's grace, given me through the working of His power" (Ephesians 3:7).

What I get to share with people in my work as a pastor has all been formed by my experience of God's grace in my life. Each sermon, small group, and meeting I lead are a reflection of the gift of grace, God's power in me.

My son Josiah loves stories. We read together all the time and we also make up stories. At bedtime one night when he was 4-years old, I started to weave a made-up tale. Many times, he gives me promptings and I need to run with it. "Tell me a story about when a butterfly crashed into hot lava," was my story prompt one time. This night though, when I started to make up a story, Josiah interrupted me.

> Josiah: "Remember we were in the car ride and driving around the parking lot at the Redlands Market, mommy?"
>
> Me: Yes.
>
> Josiah: "Remember when we drove fast and you held on and we had so much wind in our hair?"
>
> Me: Yes, I do.
>
> Josiah: "Tell me that story."

Yes, son. In the midst of the beautiful, creative stories that we read and tell, we must remember to tell our own stories. The ones that actually happen to us. Yes, my boy, I will tell the story of us. I will tell the story of what happened and what we really experienced. I want to savor that story.

It's easy to forget to tell our story. Yet, discipleship is about telling our story. We are shaped and formed by God as we share our own story with each other. Disciple-making is being willing to share our lives. In 1 Thessalonians 2:8, Paul says, "Because we loved you so much, we were delighted to share with you not only the gospel of God but our lives as well."

This is the call to discipleship: to share the gospel and to share our lives. So, on these pages, you will read about being rooted in the gospel, how God can root believers in your church or ministry or small group in the gospel of Jesus Christ. You will read about the invitation of God and the transformation by the power of the Holy Spirit through this journey. You will also read about my life. Because the gospel and my life are intertwined.

To tell God's story we must share our story.

As you lead and make space for discipleship in your church, business, small group, or your family, would you have the courage to show up and tell your own story? Yes, share the good news—we all need to hear the good news. Yet right alongside the good news, will you share your story?

Let me pause for a moment to speak to those of us who are struggling to believe. Yes, leaders, elders, pastors, administrators, and long-time members, we can all struggle at different times. Perhaps right now it feels like too much—an invisible God who wants a relationship with us. Look for a moment. Love is visible all around you. Ask God to wake you up to notice grace. Then look at the evidence in you. Whenever you want to love someone, not for something he or she can do for you, but just simply from love, whenever you forgive someone for a wrong, or you share sacrificially, these evidences show the Spirit and grace at work. Even if you don't see and don't feel what you have believed before, when you do these things, we see God in you. You evidence God's goodness.

When it feels dark and we don't know the way, hear the words of Jesus to Thomas that become words for us. Thomas had a mix of doubt and faith, confusion and confidence. Jesus said, "Blessed are those who have not seen, and yet have come to believe" (John 20:29).

Seventh-day Adventists believe that all life change starts with responding to God who loves us first. Turning towards God in response to grace.

You and I are invited into a relationship. You and I are invited to live in this love as a disciple, and to make other disciples on the journey.

"Now to Him who is able to do infinitely more than all we ask or imagine, according to His power that is at work within us" (Ephesians 3:20).

May God bless the journey before us.

CHAPTER ZERO

Making Space for God

"We want to go to God for answers, but sometimes what we get is God's presence."

NADIA BOLZ-WEBER

THE SMALL GROUP IS GATHERED in a tight circle around the audio recorder. They have been on a journey of growth and change over the last three months. They have laughed, prayed, and cried together—sharing themselves as they have grown closer. You can see by the eye contact and the affection in the room that the space between them has grown sacred. This is the last time they will be together as part of a 12-week discipleship process. The relationships will continue between them, but the group time has come to an end. Now they are taking a few moments of this last session together to record their thoughts and experiences for my doctoral research. Significant themes arise from what they share. These are some highlights.

INTEGRATION:

"This just totally transformed my walk with God… It was so good to have the creative expressions enter my devotional life… I talk to God about everything now."

SLOWING DOWN:

"I'm always running around, but God really slowed me down through this process. It was wonderful to stop and reflect on the Scripture."

SUFFERING AND COMMUNITY:

"There were trials in my life during this process, but I didn't feel alone in them, I shared them with others. It actually felt like less of a trial, even though the circumstances didn't change, because I had people that cared and I understood more about God's care for me."

FINDING PEACE:

"Now, when I surrender things to God I actually feel peace. Before, it was me telling myself that I am at peace, but now it's God telling me that I am at peace."

PRAYER AND PRAISE:

"A lot of my prayers before were focused on me and life—what I need to do. But this has helped me to focus more on praise in my prayer life. It's great to have focus on God and who He is."

RELATIONSHIP:

"I think one of the greatest blessings was the time I had with my spiritual companion."

INTIMACY:

"I fight against intimacy because I don't like getting close to people. I don't like getting close to people because I don't like getting hurt… This process just took all of that fight away."

Tears spring to my eyes when I think about the growth that I have witnessed in my own life, and in the lives of those who have participated in this and subsequent discipleship journeys that I have had the privilege of facilitating. The transformation is real and significant. Time and again, I have watched in wonder as God has grown individuals and our community.

So how did we get to this moment where we revel in the growth and changes that God has brought among and through us?

I am inviting you to begin with a glimpse of the details that make up an intentional discipleship process. This is both the beginning and the end of a process. This is both a first and a last chapter. Learning experientially is a cycle of doing and reflecting on why one does what one does. I will begin this book by describing the specifics of how a 12-week discipleship process can be implemented in a local church. Later chapters will explore the research and biblical foundations for each of the concepts and themes that you see reflected in this chapter.

The Beginning

At the start of each retreat and discipleship group, I make a speech. Inspired by several authors and teachers,[1] my words are as follows:

> We are not here to learn facts about God or how to hear God in our lives, we are going to practice together how to show up in God's presence and listen for God's voice. Our role in spiritual life is the same as our role today. Your role is to (1) show up and (2) surrender to what God is doing.
>
> I ask you to turn off your cell phones or put them on "do not disturb." You are making space in your life to spend time with God. Extended communion in God's presence takes focus. We rush so much and have days filled so much with noise that at first silence might actually be scary. I get it. Take a deep breath and trust what God is doing in you.

This is about allowing the Holy Spirit to mentor you. I have found again and again that God comes alongside you, asking questions you hadn't thought of, challenging you to think in new ways, capturing your imagination, and letting your heart soar in love.

I asked you all to bring a Bible, a journal, a pen, and a water bottle today. However, I caution you not to force yourself to think of something to write. Pray and open yourself to writing what God brings to your mind.

Don't expect to leave today a different person. This is important. You will be different, but not in the ways you might notice or expect. Let God show you where God is leading you. Sometimes we try to control everything, including the change process in our own lives!

We are creating space for God to work in our lives. God is the only one who knows what needs to happen in your life and in mine. God is the director of our process.

These words mark the beginning of a very intentional and sacred process. The planning for this process began months earlier. Here is a glimpse into how I prepared for this moment.

A Discipleship Journey

A discipleship journey is all about making space for participants to show up for the work God desires to do in their lives. I share an invitation for anyone who wants to experience growth in their relationship with God to sign up. Participants are accepted on a first-come basis through an open invitation to the church and a voluntary sign-up process on the church website. I created a promotional video for advertising the discipleship journey. This is shown in the church on Sabbath morning, typically about 4-5 weeks before the desired launch date, and is placed on the church's website and social media pages.

The individuals who sign up each year are diverse in age, race, gender, and education. They represent a diversity in spiritual maturity, including newly baptized believers, members not yet engaged in ministry, and long-time members, all wanting to grow in their relationship with God.

Spiritual Companions

Participants are paired with a spiritual companion of the same gender with whom they journey throughout the 12-week process.

I have seen God lead in this process in incredible ways, pairing people with one another who could aid their growth in ways we could never guess at the outset. I intentionally pray for this part of the process, knowing this has the potential to affect the experience on the journey dramatically. The Holy Spirit leads as participants join with me in prayer and choose a partner at the opening retreat.

At the start of each discipleship journey session there is an opening question that is discussed between the spiritual companions. This time of sharing allows them to grow closer with one another—allocating time for peer-to-peer mentoring, support, and accountability. Spiritual companions are taught how to support one another. I firmly believe, and research supports, that we grow most by encouragement and affirmation, by listening, and by being seen.[2]

Transformation comes from the presence of God, and when we engage in this process with others, we help each other become more aware of God's presence in our own lives. Spiritual Companions help us to become more aware of how God is moving and speaking in our lives. Spiritual companions accompany us on our journey with God. The space between us is sacred, not because of us, but by the very presence of God in our midst. They are a "safe space" where we are able to more freely experience the love of God. Spiritual companions learn how best to engage with the spiritual journey of another through the discipleship process and how this is modeled by the leader.

At the start of the journey, a Personal Assessment (*see Appendix*) is given to each participant, with instructions to spend two hours exploring the questions. The next week, the spiritual companions share from this assessment, showing up honestly with one another.

Small Groups

Within the class, each pair of spiritual companions finds another pair and forms a small group of four. This peer group of four people (ideally of the same gender), remains consistent throughout the discipleship process. Most classes allow for small-group time of at least 30 minutes each session and encourage the small groups to gather outside of the class setting for the purpose of spiritual growth and accountability.

All of us have made commitments to ourselves regarding many things such as exercising or eating right or devotional practices. Not unlike these other life changes, the discipleship journey is something that happens best in a community. Peter, James, and John were disciples of Jesus, not individually, but as a group. The groups covenant with one another to show up, no matter what they are feeling, and to be present with each other and with God. The small groups covenant to trust God in the process, agreeing to depend on God for answers, not needing to solve or answer one another's problems. They are committed to hearing one another.

Retreats

The discipleship journey begins with an all-day spiritual retreat. This has taken place at different locations over the years, including a Christian retreat center, a summer camp, a hotel conference room, and on a university campus. My favorite locations allow for food to be easily available at the same location, and provide ample outdoor space for participants to move between the indoors and the natural setting outside.

    The opening retreat begins at 9:00 a.m. with several worship songs and a time of prayer. The theme is "Learning to Hear God's Voice." The participants are given time to spend alone with God for each part, using only their Bible and their journals. Participants are encouraged to trust God and come into the silence, knowing and expecting that God is waiting to speak to them. After each time alone, participants are then invited back to share for one hour in their small groups, allowing approximately 15 minutes per person to process what God has been speaking to them. A one-hour break is given for lunch and fellowship time. At the close of the day, the class processes the question: "What was the most significant part about today?" Each person has the opportunity to share with the larger group. The day ends at 5:00 p.m. with a conversational-style group prayer.

    At the end of the 12-weeks, the discipleship process concludes with a second all-day spiritual retreat at the same location. The theme for this retreat is "Abide and Adore" and centers around John 15, the parable of the vine and the branches, and Mark 14:1-9, the woman who anointed Jesus at Bethany. This retreat opens with prayer and worship songs at 9:00 a.m. Scriptures from John 15 are set up by the leader on sign boards located throughout the garden area outside the meeting room doors. In other venues, Scripture sign boards have been set up around the conference room, church fellowship hall, or the campus lawn. Participants are invited to take their journals and move around from verse to verse in any order, as they are led by the Holy Spirit. Following this time, participants meet with their small groups and share how God has spoken to them.

    Next, participants explore God's presence in their past and their present.[3] They write out their major life events—joys, losses, moves, celebrations—and perhaps create a "timeline" for their lives. They ask themselves where God has worked in their past and where God is present and working in their lives right now. Participants are given time to spend alone with God, using only their journals and their Bibles. Following the time of reflection, the small groups take time to share how God led during their time.

After lunch, each person is instructed to choose one of four characters from Mark 14:1-9—the woman, Simon the Leper, a disciple, and Jesus—and to enter the reading of the Scripture from that unique perspective. After listening to God in the Word, they are then invited to share with one another in their small groups. It is powerful to witness how participants open up to one another during this experience because the relationships they share are deeper as a result of the 12-week process.

Transitioning from this time in the Word, the group is led to an art room with various supplies, including paper products, paint, clay, yarn, and markers. Participants are instructed to spend time in silence with God, listening to God answer the question, "Where do you, God, want to take me from here?" They are instructed to use whatever art supplies they wish to share where God wants to take them from there. Each person then shares with the entire group what they created and how God spoke to them. The revelations of God's direction are astonishing and beautiful. For many, using the art supplies in this process opens them up spiritually and allows them to go deeper with God. The day concludes with the spiritual companions anointing each other with olive oil and praying for one another in affirmation of the specific direction God showed during the previous session. The group gathers for one last time in conversational prayer before dismissing at 5:00 p.m.[4]

Weekly Meeting

Following the first all-day retreat, the class meets once a week for two hours. I have found the day of the week changes depending on the church schedule. However, the time that has worked best has consistently been 7:00-9:00 pm. The sessions focus on the eight calls of God detailed in chapter nine, and three foundational values from chapters five and eight: relationship with God, community, and purpose, also referred to as witness and service.

Experiential activities are a part of each class, in addition to activity suggestions given at the end of each class so that members are able to practice what they are learning throughout the next week. Participants are invited to read one verse per day in the Gospel of John throughout the discipleship journey. When participants share with their spiritual companions at the start of the meeting, they are encouraged to share their gospel of John experiences after the opening question.

Each class time involves a balance of time alone, one-on-one reflection with spiritual companions, four-person peer mentoring groups, and larger group interaction. The eight calls of God—some might call them spiritual habits or disciplines—are explored during this time (more on this in chapter nine). Content is taught, and then members are given time to experience and practice how the lesson connects with their current place in their spiritual journey. The discipleship journey time focuses on process and involvement, engaging each member in the experiential learning triad: knowing, being, and doing, as shared in chapter eight.

Throughout the years, I have found that sending email reminders and text messages to participants encourages continued engagement in the process. Leaders are facilitating a journey that is constructing new habits. Reminders help participants learn these new habits.

Community Building

Intentional community building is incorporated into the discipleship journey in order to facilitate further relationship growth. This takes place at lunch time on the two retreat days, and through a discipleship group fellowship dinner, which takes place midway through the journey at my home. The evening fellowship is typically from 6:00-10:00 p.m. on a Saturday night and includes dinner, games, dessert, and conversation. This time allows for an integration for participants between the self that is processing deeply in the discipleship journey and the self that shows up for games on a Saturday night.

Length

The 12-week length was selected for this discipleship journey as a manageable length of time that people can commit to, while still allowing crucial time for growth and depth of relationship to form among participants. Discipleship expert Bill Hull states that small groups average around 40 days in length and that groups need to meet for longer in order to form together as a group.[5] This length is also supported by the witness of practical ministry discovered during my phone interviews with pastors whose churches excel in discipleship. These churches averaged 8-10 weeks for their small groups.[6] In my experience, the 12-week length afforded time necessary for group cohesion and bonding, as well as teaching and forming new spiritual habits.

Though there are good reasons for selecting the 12-week length for this discipleship journey, other researchers indicate that a longer time as a discipleship group is preferred over the shorter length of time. Greg Ogden recommends that discipleship groups stay together through at least a one-year process.[7] Stanley and Willits keep participants in their community discipleship groups consistent through an 18-24 month covenant. Bill Hull recognizes that groups become most effective around six months, or at their twenty-fifth meeting.[9]

In the context of the Seventh-day Adventist Church, I have found that a commitment to longer than 12-weeks for a stand-alone discipleship journey is challenging to implement. The weight of evidence leans towards a longer time frame for maximum growth and transformation. This is best seen in the Sabbath School group. Many Sabbath School classes have been together for 5, 10, or 15+ years. The depth of relationship and life change can be seen in healthy classes. In the Adventist context, it's important to remember that growth continues for many participants by being part of a group of this kind.

Size and Make-up of the Group

Every time I have implemented the discipleship journey through voluntary sign up, the groups varied in race, age, gender, and socio-economic status, as well as maturity of faith and relationship with Christ. The goal is to maintain diversity, while being intentional about recruiting leaders who will then be able to replicate the process of discipleship by starting a group themselves. A leader must experience the discipleship journey to know firsthand the closeness and transformation that takes place. As they go through the entire process led by the pastor, they are more equipped to be able to lead in that process with other believers.

Regarding group size, I recommend that groups have an even number of participants, either 12 or 16 people. After over a dozen times of implementing the discipleship curriculum, my preferred group size is 12 participants. A group size of 12 affords for three small groups of four participants each. This smaller size allows for deeper bonding in relationships, and therefore greater change in the lives of participants. The smaller size also contributes to a higher level of timeliness and faithfulness in attendance, because one person's presence is greatly missed by the spiritual companion and the small group. During Spiritual Companion or Small Group time, the leader/facilitator is in constant prayer, asking for the Holy Spirit to work and interceding by name for each of the participants while slowly walking around the room. The leader is not paired up with a Spiritual Companion or in a Small Group so that they are free to pray and partner with God. They may observe the group and create a prayerful space during these times.

Hands-on Service

Participants are encouraged to get involved at a higher level in service and witnessing. The discipleship journey group provides hands-on opportunities for service, allowing participants to engage in both service and witnessing.

    Before the discipleship session on service, the leader/facilitator prepares a list of service opportunities with descriptions for the small groups to choose from. Some ideas may include collecting sleeping bags for homeless veterans, starting a Bible study, creating care kits for those without homes, volunteering in a children's Sabbath School classroom, reading stories to school-age children, knitting prayer shawls, picking up trash in a park, writing/mailing encouragement cards, volunteering at a soup kitchen or food pantry, preparing a church mailing for the community, and so on. You'll want to see what is available in your community. Keep in mind that some options should be less action-oriented so that, depending how able-bodied people are, there are some projects that can be done sitting down. During the session, small groups review the list of projects and decide on one to engage in together.

Conclusion and Implications

I've seen through research and experience that a discipleship journey in the local church is most effective when it embraces an experiential model of learning, which equally values knowing, being, and doing in the life of the follower of Jesus. What emerged through prayer, research, and the process of implementation are the following five goals that form the structural framework for the discipleship process:

A. **Provide opportunity for connection with God:** By practicing the eight calls (devotional habits), participants will learn to listen to God by connecting in a personal relationship and by being transformed in God's presence.

B. **Develop community:** By teaching, one-on-one mentoring, small groups, and process orientation, the groundwork for healthy relationships is established.

C. **Inspire a life of purpose:** By coaching and instructing individuals to serve others and share Jesus in their sphere of influence.

D. **Emphasize life-long transformation:** By encouraging individuals that transformation takes time—highlighting the importance of abiding in Jesus throughout the transformation process, which lasts for a lifetime.

E. **Simplify discipleship practice:** By intentionally teaching the devotional habits and inviting participants to disciple others they know, this process demystifies what it means to disciple others.

As each of these priorities are kept in focus through prayer and the leadership of the Holy Spirit, individuals will experience change in their lives and will begin to live differently in the world. Inward transformation leads to mission orientation.

May you have courage to allow God to direct the growth in your life and in the lives of those you lead.

May you find companions for the journey, mutually investing in one another's lives.

May you make space for the work of discipleship God is doing and desires to do in your midst.

Discussion Questions

1. At the beginning of the chapter is a list of quotes from participants of the discipleship process, highlighting significant themes. Which of these resonates most with you? Why?
2. Which part of the discipleship process makes you the most excited? The most uncomfortable?
3. Which of the five goals that form the structural framework for the discipleship process does your church or community already excel at? In which area do you see room for growth?

CHAPTER ONE

You Will Be Like a Tree

*"When life is sweet, say thank you and celebrate.
And when life is bitter, say thank you and grow."*

SHAUNA NIEQUIST

What if I told you that God could radically transform your life and ministry through ordinary spiritual habits, but that the days, months, and years may not feel radical at all?

What if I told you that discipleship is the most important area of ministry you can focus on, but that many times, everything else will feel more important and more urgent?

What if I told you that transformation is possible, but that it's less about what we do and more about making space for God to do the work God is already doing?

I have been on a journey with God that has transformed my life and ministry. In 2010, I began my Doctor of Ministry degree in

Discipleship and Biblical Spirituality. It was through this process that I was able to reflect on what has sustained and anchored me over the last 25 years since I came to faith as a teenager. I was able to put words to God's work in my own life and what has been most meaningful in my ministry. Looking back and naming the ways God had been effectively growing disciples through my ministry, as well as naming the things that didn't work have been a critical part of my learning.

On the journey to complete my degree, I wrote a 12-week discipleship experience for the local church. I have now implemented this curriculum over a dozen times in the past 10 years. It has grown and I have grown. I have pastored for 20 years in three states. I have lived "up close" with the joys and challenges of ministry. I have suffered. I have developed resolve and grit and perseverance. I have seen God's glory, even with wounds and an aching heart. I have seen God's faithfulness. All of this has changed me and has changed what I bring to the discipleship journey.

Like a Tree

Growing up in the Northwestern part of the United States, I have a life-long love of trees. I spent time backpacking and hiking in the forests, breaking off pine needles and rubbing them in my hands to smell the fresh pine scent. I learned the names of the trees, counted their rings, and played beneath their branches. You've heard of a "tree hugger?" Yes, that's me! I am from Washington, after all! I remember being afraid as a young child, perhaps 6 or 7 years old, and crawling underneath the towering Douglas Fir by our home. I leaned against the trunk and felt secure, even in the damp, cold afternoon.

When I became a Christian, I gravitated to the image of the tree of life. Over the years I have collected paintings and wall hangings of this imagery made from various materials from different countries around the world. Whether created with rough rope, watercolor, stained glass, or embroidery, this image connects with me deeply.

About the Torah or Wisdom, Proverbs states, "It is a tree of life to all who grasp it, and whoever holds on to it is happy; its ways are ways of pleasantness, and all its paths are peace" (Proverbs 3:17-18).

The Torah refers to the Pentateuch or books of Moses, which are the first five books of the Bible. Yet, it also refers to the Jewish understanding of their origins. The Torah, or the Tree of Life, was an anchor for the Jewish people. The story of how God created and called them, held them through trials and hardship, and covenanted with them to embody a way of being which honored God in all areas of life, morality, religion, and civic duty. The law of God was pictured as a tree—a tree of life—rooting the people of God in God's story, which was actually their story, as well. The Word of God was never just the Word; it was the story of God and God's people, a shared story.

Then the time comes for the redemptive purposes of God to be made visible. Jesus comes incarnate in human flesh—walking and talking, eating and drinking—living among us. Fully God and fully human, Jesus comes to us dependent, vulnerable, and enfleshed. Jesus didn't come to abolish this law (the tree of life), but to fulfill it (Matthew 5:17). God brought the tree of life to full fruitfulness through God's own gift of love in Jesus. Jesus connected us with this Word and lived its significance in ways we couldn't picture before. Jesus' life, and then his death on the tree, brought life, hope, and healing. Jesus rooted us in our identity and God's story, which it turns out, is our story too. In a world tired, suffering, and distracted, a life is still the best way to show what God is like. I believe, as Eugene Peterson says, that the Word of God can be lived.[1]

Roots

We humans have always yearned for roots, to know where we come from. The phenomenon of genealogies and ancestry sites highlight this inner need to know. Send in a sample and get back the full report about who you are and where you come from. Why do we do this? We long for roots. We want to understand where we come from because maybe if we get that, we can know where we're going.

With so much information and the speed we live with each day, we need to know who we are and why we are the way we are to root us. Our ancestry, we hope, will help to ground us. Like a tree.

People have often asked me, "How did you make it through what you've been through? What allowed you to be able to go through this and emerge on the other side?" The short answer is, by the mercy and grace of God alone. How? God has rooted me deeply in Jesus and in my identity. Through it all—discrimination, death, rejection, loss, and heartbreak—I have found roots in my Creator.

The biblical story of humanity began at a tree. Pain and heartache started there. The law, pictured as a tree, was not able to be kept and we fell short. Then, in Jesus, our redemption came on a tree. The law was enlivened and we were empowered to live this Word with strength beyond our own. Our story ends, or really begins again, at a tree—gathered as we will be around a tree of life for all eternity. In this one image is our shared identity, calling, and hope. Deep roots, deep love, deep calling.

"You will be like a tree planted by streams of water" (Psalm 1:3).

This is discipleship. *Deep Calling* is a journey of becoming more rooted in God, for we are all like trees, sinking our roots deep into the love of God.

As a person and as a leader, my hope is that as you read this book you will hear the invitation of God to open up your life to the process of transformation that God is working in you through ordinary life habits, see the supreme importance of discipleship in the church, have a clear and simple path to implementing a discipleship group in your church, and experience the bridge between a reflective, prayerful life and an active, missional life—the peace and stillness that leads to making a difference in the world.

It isn't about becoming more sanctified or "spiritual" by our own efforts, as if that were something we could control. Instead, the discipleship journey is about learning how to trust. Trust the mystery of what God is doing in you. That's first and foremost. Before you and I run off with application to the local church, ministry, conference, or group where we serve, we must let the Holy Spirit speak into our own lives. How does God want to root us?

Then, trust the mystery of what God is doing in your ministry. As you and I abide in Jesus, there is fruit we don't know about that is growing and coming. There is more that God is calling you and people in your area of influence to experience. The single biggest impact you can have on those you are discipling is to share an understanding that **this is a life-long process, not a destination**. The journey is about learning how to lean into trust in God and surrender to the work God is doing in our lives.

I am not an expert. Yes, I did earn the Doctor of Ministry degree in Discipleship and Biblical Spirituality. Yes, I have loved implementing discipleship groups through all these years. Yet, what I have learned is that what matters most is having the courage to make space for what the Holy Spirit wants to do. God desires to grow the people of God; my role is to respond and guard space for this work in my own life and in the lives of others. This work you have in your hands is no exception. I don't have all the answers, but I've found that I don't need to. What God asks of you and me is to be faithful. This book is the next step for me in seeking to share faithfully as God calls me to share. It is my hope that God will use this process to lead you to the next faithful step for you and for your ministry.

I'm here praying for you, cheering for you! You see, we all need you to be fully you. Our world and the church are depending on your living deeply from rootedness in God, answering that deep call to communion with God. Then, from that place of rootedness, for you to live from the gifts and calling that are uniquely yours.

I am grateful for you.
Thanks for being a partner on the journey.
Thanks be to God for this amazing love and grace.

Discussion Questions:

1. Which of the three questions at the beginning of this chapter inspires you the most?
2. What has rooted you in your own discipleship journey?
3. In what ways is God calling you to trust the mystery of what God is doing in your life and ministry?

CHAPTER TWO

What is Discipleship?

*"We must be ready to allow ourselves
to be interrupted by God."*

DIETRICH BONHOEFFER

YOU'VE HEARD IT SAID that if you can just find the right process, you'll keep people in the church. I believe that as long as we are dealing with people, we will deal with mistakes and failures and suffering. This means that we don't have the power to "keep" people anywhere. Not much hope in that, right? Actually there is, and that hope is found in relationship and in trust with Jesus.

From the moment I heard about Him, Jesus captured my heart. I learned that God desired to be with me and this changed my life and shifted my priorities. I came to believe in and experience a God who sought me out, accepted me as I am, and, over time, is transforming me. When I first believed, I was invited to live out ways that connected me to God and I began prayer journaling, reading Scripture devotionally, sharing my story (witnessing), and sitting in stillness with God. Over the years since coming to faith as a teenager, these habits have grown, changed, and deepened. As I have followed Jesus, living in a relationship with God, I have experienced benefits. The blessing of peace of mind, purpose, and passion for a life of service; joy in the midst of difficulties; and a sense of security in the love of God. It's not easy. In fact, some days sitting in silent prayer is difficult and the distractions frequent. Yet, time and again, God comes. God's presence is what makes the difference in my life. This is the Christian disciple's journey.

This is something many have experienced. There is beauty in the diversity of how God meets with us and walks with us. Sadly, this is not the experience for all. Some have come to God because they were convicted of the truth and they knew they needed to follow it. While that was a meaningful step in their lives, they were told little of where to go from there. They didn't take the next steps of learning how to live in a relationship with God and join in the work of God. They have not experienced for themselves the sweetness of the presence of God and the invitation to join the purpose of God in the world. This relational and experiential void can lead to a propensity towards legalism and fear for some, or growing lukewarm and complacent for others. Still others walk away altogether when something new comes along.

The majority of Seventh-day Adventist churches in the North American Division are in a state of plateau or decline, begging the question: Has an emphasis on "having the truth" resulted in the development of devoted disciples? Do people with orthodox biblical information automatically become people who are Christ-like, living Jesus' love and mission in the world? Does the church have a discipleship strategy that is working? While some would say that the primary purpose for the existence of the Seventh-day Adventist Church is the transmission of right knowledge, Scripture suggests that a healthy church lives and breathes through a love relationship with Jesus. It is this personal encounter, and not merely information about God, which in turn draws others to want to experience

Jesus for themselves. The church exists to *be* God's presence in the world, teaching people to become followers who are in a relationship with Jesus and with one another (John 13:35). Could it be that an over-emphasis on right information in the Seventh-day Adventist Church, to the neglect of teaching the primacy of how to have a relationship with Jesus, has caused members to become malnourished in the area of spiritual growth? The fact that hearts and lives lack transformation is seen in the bitter fruit of a lack of assurance of the love of God, spiritual pride, disregard for mission, and a lack of forgiveness, among other fruits.

So… What is Discipleship?

I was speaking on discipleship at a conference recently and I asked the group a question: "What is discipleship?" A young woman said, "I went to a whole weekend on discipleship at my church." Feeling hopeful I said again, "So, what is discipleship?" She looked back at me and said, "I don't even know."

Somehow in the midst of all we are doing and all we believe, we can miss the very thing we are called to. *Deep Calling* is a discipleship journey focused on making space for what matters most.

Let's start with the basics. Seventh-day Adventists are Christians. A Christian is a person devoted to following Christ. Discipleship is a word we use to describe the process of growth in Christ. Discipleship is a posture of learning. To be a disciple is to be a life-long student and follower of Jesus. Discipleship is a relationship, devotion, journey, a new perspective, abiding, and a "Spirit imbued" life. Discipleship is the process of transformation or formation in the life of the believer.

Christianity has placed an emphasis on receiving the gift of salvation, often at the loss of emphasizing the sanctification journey that follows. Adventists have placed a greater emphasis on sanctification, often at the expense of the security of salvation in

Jesus. Discipleship is both justification (receiving salvation as a free gift) and sanctification (the ongoing growth and life transformation) that God desires to work in the life of each believer.

I come to this journey with a few presuppositions—core beliefs that guide the process. I believe God is personal and loving and active in human life through Jesus and the Holy Spirit. I believe God desires close communion through the means provided to us: the Scriptures (the Word), the Church (community of Christ), the Creation (this world), and the Call (an experience with God that arises from our partnership with God's work in the world). I believe we are called to keep central a relationship with Jesus, the love of the Father, and the fellowship of the Holy Spirit. All other beliefs move from a relationship with a Triune God.

Discipleship in the Church

In the calling of His first disciples, Jesus invited them (a) to be with Him and (b) to learn how to fish for people (Mark 1:17-18). A transformational relationship with Jesus serves as a catalyst for evangelism. The two callings go hand in hand. Many biblical examples could be cited to demonstrate this connection between relationship and evangelism. For the purposes of this study, I'll explore three here: the Samaritan woman, the disciples at Pentecost, and the conversion of Paul.

In the first example, Jesus met a Samaritan woman at the well, and in this initial encounter Christ revealed to her that He was the promised Messiah. Jesus also showed that He knew who she was, and still accepted her. She could not contain her joy and immediately ran to the town to share the news with others. Many were converted because of her testimony (John 4:1-42). For this woman, seeing God and experiencing love and acceptance, led to a missional witness.

In the second example, the disciples were in an upper room

waiting for the Holy Spirit before going out to give witness to the resurrection of the Lord (Acts 1:4-5). When they experienced the power of the Holy Spirit in their lives, they shared Jesus and 3,000 joined the church in one day (Acts 2)! The presence of the Holy Spirit in the lives of the disciples resulted in missional activity.

In the final example, Saul, who became Paul, experienced a dramatic conversion on the road to Damascus. He met Jesus for himself. From that encounter, he was changed from a persecutor of the church to an apostle of Jesus Christ. Paul began witnessing and teaching others about Jesus (Acts 9:19-22). Inward transformation became a catalyst for worldwide mission activity. The common theme in each of these stories is this: An experience with Jesus leads to sharing God with others.

In these biblical examples, we can note several practical features that must be included in a discipleship process for the local church. First, there must be an emphasis on a personal experience with God, which involves connecting in a relationship. In this discipleship process this is primarily experienced through the eight calls, or devotional practices. Second, time must be given for God to transform the life of the believer inwardly. It's not easy, but discipleship involves waiting for a work in us that we don't control or manufacture. We must recognize that the discipleship journey is a process, a work God is doing in us. It is not solely about learning content, but instead opening up to transformation. Third, one-on-one mentoring (as Jesus did with the woman at the well and with Paul), growth in community (as Jesus did with the twelve original disciples), and shared experience (as with the believers at Pentecost) are helpful learning models that lead to inward change. Fourth, and finally, the discipleship process must focus on both a relationship with Jesus and an active joining in God's mission. Time spent with Jesus leads to action in the world in the unique ways God has gifted each disciple.

The following four features are what make up the foundation

of this discipleship process for the local church: (1) Focusing on a personal experience with Jesus, (2) allowing consistent time for transformation, (3) process orientation and community context, and (4) joining Jesus in His mission. We will explore these in greater depth below.

Personal Experience With Jesus

Every person who serves as a positive spiritual example in both the Old and New Testaments had an encounter with God that changed his or her life. In the Old Testament, Joseph, Moses, and David stand out as prominent examples of individuals who encountered God and had the trajectory of their lives altered. In the New Testament, Peter, John, Mary, and others all had life-altering connections with Jesus Christ that changed them forever.

This personal experience with Jesus must be the Source of transformation, strength, and action in the life of the believer. Jesus emphasized the necessity of abiding in Him, stating that apart from Him, the believer is unable to do anything (John 15:5). A discipleship process in the local church must champion this emphasis, lifting Jesus up and allowing Jesus to draw people to Himself (John 12:32). In a world where many things compete for attention, the local church discipleship process must advocate for the primacy of a personal experience with Jesus for each individual follower.

Time for Transformation

Jesus believed that He needed to spend time with the disciples in order for change to happen. The discipleship process cannot be boiled down into a pamphlet, tract, or even a book. Discipleship is an experience, modeled and lived in community. Has the church lost the point when she substitutes time spent modeling what it looks like to follow Jesus, with a focus on the transmission of information, apart from relationship?

Discipleship is learned in the context of relationship with God and other believers. Discipleship is the process whereby individuals allow God to transform their lives through time spent with Jesus and the practice of what God has taught them. Knowledge is essential to the process, but disciples must allow God to move them from knowledge, to reflection, to action. This takes time and is the process of yielding to God for the work that only God can do. As Eugene Peterson says, the question of the disciple is not, "what do I do" but "what is God doing?"[1]

Process-Orientation

The Scriptures contain evidence that Jesus was process-oriented with the disciples. For example, when Jesus taught His disciples something they failed to grasp the meaning of, He would often repeat the teaching in a different way so they could understand it. Jesus repeated the prediction of His death three times (Matthew 16:21; 17:22-23; 20:17-19). Jesus was patient with the lack of understanding the disciples exhibited (John 14:1-14), and there were times when the disciples did not understand a lesson until much later (John 2:22). In the Upper Room, as Jesus washed the disciple's feet, He told them clearly, "You do not realize now what I am doing, but later you will understand" (John 13:7, 19). This reveals that Jesus was teaching with a process in mind that extended beyond the current interaction. Lastly, on the road to Emmaus, Jesus encountered two disciples and taught them the Scriptures (Luke 24:25-27, 44-45). These were disciples who had heard this instruction before, but still did not see the meaning. Jesus' response was to teach it again. Rather than moving on to new content, Jesus paid careful attention to their level of comprehension and adjusted His teachings accordingly. Jesus' teaching was typically grounded in the practical experiences which were taking place in His disciple's lives.

The primary goal of practicing discipleship in community is to create space for listening to the Holy Spirit and learning from one another. The goal is not to rush through content in order to make it through, but to go at the pace of the individuals involved in the process. Just as Jesus used process learning with His disciples, He also used one-on-one mentoring, small groups, and shared experience with the 12 original apostles to deepen the impression of the instruction. With the discipleship process outlined in this book, believers do the same when they journey together as disciples, creating space for God to help them understand and practice more fully the teachings of Jesus. The discipleship journey involves learning in quietness, away from distractions. As individuals listen deeply to God, they also listen and become connected with the people around them.

In the discipleship process, there is no substitute for the slow transformation that takes place in the Presence of God and with one another. No pamphlet, no "how-to" guide, or video series can rush the molding of the Spirit and the formation process that God directs.

Joining Jesus in Mission

Disciples are those who are with Jesus and who make disciples. As stated above, Jesus invited the disciples to be with Him and to learn how to "fish for people" (Mark 1:17-18). Both were essential to their role as disciples. In each of the scriptural examples given above, individuals met Jesus and proceeded to share Jesus with others. Essential to the discipleship process is an understanding of this emphasis and practical instruction in mission, both witness and service. Foundational to the process of discipleship is the fact that a personal relationship with Jesus always leads to greater purpose. This mission orientation is the act of joining Jesus in His work in the world. For a local church process, this means helping believers understand their giftedness, their purpose, and how to live out their calling in the world.

It is my conviction that experiencing the process of discipleship can change the way we stay connected and grow in God. I long for all those who join the Seventh-day Adventist Church, either by birth or conversion, to be led in what it looks like to grow in God. Each believer is called to focus on a relationship with Jesus, to allow time for transformation, to realize that discipleship is a process, not an event or "arrival," and to learn how to join God in the work of the Kingdom.

> *May Jesus capture your heart and guide your life.*
>
> *May God bless you to discover one way you are called to grow in Christ where you are now.*
>
> *May God give you courage to create spaces where others can experience growth in Christ.*

Discussion Questions:

1. What are the practices or habits that have been most meaningful for you in your growth as a disciple?
2. What is one way you are called to grow in Christ right now?
3. How is God leading you to disciple others?

CHAPTER THREE

The Experience of Discipleship

"There are only three ways to teach a child. The first is by example, the second is by example, the third is by example."

ALBERT SCHWEITZER

WHEN RAISING KIDS, the goal is to help them grow into independence. Moms and dads are encouraged to keep perspective by parenting with the end in mind. If you want a healthy relationship with your adult child someday, parent toward independence.

Kids share this desire with their parents, starting as soon as they can speak. "Mine" and "Me do it" are phrases of little ones far from independent, but desiring it all the same. My little girl, who is not yet two, often says, "Ava do it" with insistence.

We marvel at watching kids learn to feed themselves, dress, and tie their own shoes. It's incredible to witness the transformation of growth. If all is well developmentally, kids grow more independent as they age.

As kids become teenagers and adults who function more independently, they learn another crucial lesson: interdependence.

Emotional maturity is this ability to be both dependent and independent—to live in the tension of independence (self-sufficiency) and interdependence (needing others).

We get so accustomed to this trajectory of growth, it's no wonder we struggle when it comes to our relationship with God. To grow up in Christ is to grow in our trust and our willingness to be dependent. God told Paul, "My strength is perfected in your weakness" (2 Corinthians 12:9). Discipleship is about making space to grow in dependence on God, rather than in our independence, and at the same time being willing to live in interdependence with the body of Christ—the believers around us. Maturity in our journey with God recognizes our inability to do life alone.

Discipleship

The word *disciple* comes from the Greek word μαθητεύω *(mathēteúō)* which means follower, learner, apprentice, or pupil. Jesus called the first disciples to follow Him (Matthew 4:19; 9:9; Mark 1:17; 2:14; Luke 5:10-11, 27-28). Later, in the book of Acts, the title "disciple" is used for all those who repented, believed, and followed Jesus through their testimony (Acts 6:2, 7; 11:26). Use of the word "disciple" in the New Testament is not exclusive to followers of Jesus. Examples include the disciples of John and the disciples of the Pharisees (Mark 2:18; Luke 5:33; Matthew 22:16), the disciples of Moses (John 9:28), as well as the apostle Paul, who was a disciple of Gamaliel (Acts 5:34; 22:3).

The Jewish concept of discipleship emphasizes the relationship between the rabbi (master) and the disciple (student). The disciple was to seek to *know* what the master knew, in addition to *doing* as the master did. The Jewish understanding of discipleship centered around the entire life being devoted to the rabbi—complete dependence.[1] Although the word "disciple" occurs only once in the Old Testament (Isaiah 8:16), the Old Testament parallel to discipleship is the concept of the covenant relationship with God (Genesis 12:1-3; 13:14-17; 28:12-15; Exodus 13:21-22; Leviticus 26:12; Deuteronomy 29:1-29). God called Israel into a relationship, which necessitated choosing God over all others (1 Kings 18:21) and serving God with complete devotion (Deuteronomy 10:12-13; 4:1-14; 1 Samuel 12:14). In both the Old Testament (Isaiah 43:10), as well as in the New Testament (Acts 1:8), God empowers human beings as witnesses. This relationship between God and God's people would showcase God's goodness, transform the people of God, and invite others into a covenant relationship (Genesis 12:1-3; Deuteronomy 4; 1 Kings 8:58-61). It is this relational pattern of dependence that the New Testament carries into the understanding of discipleship.

A Call to be With Jesus

God's relationship to us through Jesus is highlighted in the title given to Him in the book of Matthew, "The virgin will conceive and give birth to a son, and they will call him Immanuel, which means 'God with us'" (Matthew 1:23). In the deepest meaning of the Old Testament covenant, God had now joined in relationship with humanity through Jesus Christ.[2]

Jesus' ministry started with the end in mind. Jesus' purpose was clear: through His life, death, and resurrection, Jesus would bring abundant life to the world. Jesus knew that His time on earth was limited, and this informed ministry. Immediately following His baptism, which signaled the commencement of His public ministry, Jesus called disciples. In addition to sharing teaching, miracles, and ministry with the masses that would follow, Jesus chose to invest specifically in disciples who would follow Him everywhere He went. Jesus decided to pour Himself into the lives of these individuals, leaving them with the mission to touch and reach the world through dependence on the power of the Holy Spirit (Acts 1:8).

How did Matthew, John, Peter, Andrew, and the others become

disciples of Jesus? Jesus invited them (see Matthew 4:19; Mark 1:17; Luke 5:1-11; John 1:35-51). How were these ordinary men transformed to be like Jesus and carry the gospel to all the world? Mark recounts that "He appointed twelve that they might *be with him* and that he might send them out to preach" (Mark 3:14). The first calling of the disciples was to be with Jesus. From being with Jesus, the disciples were transformed. Their calling was personal, for Jesus called each one of them uniquely. Their primary focus was to spend time in His presence, and in so doing, join in the mission of God in the world.

What can be learned about the discipleship process through the lived example of Jesus? Jesus spent three and a half years of everyday life with those chosen to follow. It is easy to ignore the significance of this fact. The disciples' learning extended beyond the preaching and teaching of Jesus, to the time spent in His presence on an everyday basis.

The disciples were invited to practice preaching, performing miracles, and casting out demons, yet this was all done in the context of being in a relationship with Jesus. The act of being in a relationship with Jesus, growing in their dependence on Him, was the only way that the disciples were able to be transformed into His likeness in heart and in action (Luke 6:40; 1 Timothy 4:7b; 2 Corinthians 3:18; Romans 12:1-2).

As present day disciples approach the Christian life and seek to help others become disciples of Jesus, we must remember the heart of our calling. A. W. Tozer says, "The presence of God is the central fact of Christianity. At the heart of the Christian message is God."[3] Following Jesus is about spending time in God's presence and developing a relationship.

Ellen White expresses the believer's need of Jesus in words that make central this relational experience of the disciple. "The very first outbreathing of the soul in the morning should be for the presence of Jesus. 'Without Me,' He says, 'ye can do nothing.' It is Jesus that we need; His light, His life, His spirit, must be ours continually. We need Him every hour."[4] In Jesus is all the abundance of God—light, life, and spirit—and all that is needed to live a transformed life. We are called to live a life of dependence on Jesus.

God is the Focus of Discipleship

The Scriptures insist that a relationship with God is the center of the faith experience, the cornerstone upon which all other beliefs and doctrines rest. Jesus is Savior (Titus 3:4-7), Lord (John 20:28, 8:58), the only way to the Father (John 14:6), mediator (1 Timothy 2:5; Hebrews 9:15), friend (John 15:15), truth (John 14:6-7), and the one voice heard above all others (John 10:27-28). The author of Hebrews declares, "Let us fix our eyes on Jesus, the author and perfecter of our faith" (Hebrews 12:2).

Jesus invites us to see our dependence on God with this image. "I am the vine; you are the branches. If you remain in me and I in you, you will bear much fruit; apart from me you can do nothing" (John 15:5). The first calling of a disciple is to abide in God as in the vine (John 15:1-11). Fruit will grow in the life of the disciple as the disciple learns to remain in God (Galatians 5:22-25).

In the same way the first disciples were called to be with Jesus and to live in dependence upon Him, so every disciple is called to do the same. In the act of following after Jesus, the disciple is called to rely on God for transformation. Action and obedience are done in response to love, and not from compulsion or fear.

In John 6:68, "Simon Peter answered him, 'Lord, to whom shall we go? You have the words of eternal life.'" Peter was compelled to follow Jesus because he found Jesus to be all that he wanted and unlike anyone he had ever met—the only source of life. I've found this to be true in my own life. Even in the hardest times, I declare, "There is nowhere else I can go. I have found life in you."

The Apostle Paul declared that the primary goal of his life was to know Jesus, and to experience His sufferings and resurrection (Philippians 3:10-11). This was his singular purpose and hope, which he pressed towards during the course of his life and ministry. "For I resolved to know nothing while I was with you except Jesus Christ and him crucified" (1 Corinthians 2:2). For Paul, knowing Jesus was everything.

It is important to clarify what is meant by *knowing*, referenced above. Tozer helps to define this understanding in his book, *Keys to a Deeper Life*.

> When the apostle cried *that I may know Him*, he uses the word *know* not in its intellectual, but in its experiential sense. We must look for the meaning – not to the mind but to the heart. Theological knowledge is knowledge about God. While this is indispensable it is not sufficient. It bears the same relation to man's spiritual need as a well does to the need of his physical body. It is not the rock-lined pit for which the dusty traveler longs, but the sweet, cool water that flows up from it. It is not the intellectual knowledge about God that quenches man's ancient heart-thirst, but the Person and Presence of God Himself. These come to us through Christian doctrine, but they are more than doctrine. Christian truth is designed to lead us to God, not to serve as a substitute for God.[5]

Tozer aptly points out that theological knowledge is essential to the Christian life. Without knowledge gained from the Word of God, the Christian would not have an understanding of this God they are following. Knowledge alone is not enough; it must lead the individual to a heart-knowing, a relationship with God. It is imperative that these two points be maintained in tandem, for with one or the other missing, the church will find herself lacking either vitality or stability.

This heart-knowing is seen in the Old Testament psalms.

"As the deer pants for water so my soul pants for you my God" (Psalm 42:1). The psalmist describes the longing for God as something as basic as a profound thirst for water. This is the disciple's need for God, focusing on the LORD as the center of life. Again the psalmist declares, "My soul thirsts for you, my whole body longs for you" (Psalm 63:1). In the life of the disciple, God is their longing and completion. Jesus is the center which connects everything else in life.

Discipleship Today: People After God's Heart

To Abraham, God said—all people will be blessed through you (Genesis 12). In John 20:21, Jesus said, "As the Father sent me so I send you."

Throughout history, God was about raising up a people, a community seeking after God's heart. In each generation, God had a people. Some of the people God chose were pretty unlikely choices. Now, God's goal is the same as it was then: raise up a people of God who seek after God with all their heart, pursue God together in community, and serve and love in the context of where they live. Disciples of Jesus who show what it looks like to live the ways of God today, living in dependence on the one forming and transforming their lives.

What concerns me is not just what happens on Sabbath, or how you and I preach and teach, or how much we like what happens in our churches. What concerns me is how we, as the people of God, are living on Monday. In our Monday-through-Friday lives, what does it look like to live as disciples? Are we living dependent on God's grace as we sit down at our desks to work or clock in for the day? What does it look like to live as a disciple where you live? A disciple is a learner, a follower, a student of God's love. The learning comes in the moments, hours, days, weeks, and years of following—in all the everyday, ordinary moments.

Reading a menu is fundamentally different than tasting a meal. Listening to people describe their travels is different than traveling yourself. Hearing people tell you what they heard at the concert is different than hearing the symphony play.

It's ridiculous if we think people could experience the same thing we have by just telling them about it, right? That I could expect words to capture the taste of food. Or hearing something second-hand be the same as the adventure or concert. Words cannot equal experience. So it is with discipleship and with God's love. We grow in God by our experience. We must live it. Likewise, our invitation to others is not to hear and to know alone. The invitation is to experience. Learned dependence and relationship with the One who created us and recreates us.

There are no words adequate to describe to you what it's like to share my own experience with God and have it connect with others and move them deeply. I can't describe to you what it's like when someone says, "I wouldn't have come back to church if it wasn't for you—you made me feel welcome here." I can't describe what it's like when the worst pain I've been through somehow gets translated into empathy and love for someone else who's going through it, too. I can't describe what it's like to notice or hear about a need and be the one who gets to fill that need.

God doesn't want us to rely on a secondhand word about a relationship with God or joining Jesus in His work in the world. We are invited to join in ourselves and to make space for others to experience the same. This is discipleship—an invitation to follow God on the adventure of growing in trust and dependence.

May you, disciple of God, grow in dependence on God and interdependence in the Body of Christ.

May you be unwilling to settle for a second-hand story, instead pursuing a personal experience.

May you experience the blessing of satisfaction in God alone, the One who first pursued you.

Discussion Questions:

1. Which biblical example of discipleship resonated with you the most? Why?
2. In addition to doing ministry and church life, how can we invite people to be with Jesus as a disciple?
3. When in your life have you experienced a distinct difference between theological-knowing and heart-knowing?

CHAPTER FOUR

All Are Invited

"Whoever you are, you are human. Wherever you are, you live in the world, which is just waiting for you to notice the holiness in it."

BARBARA BROWN TAYLOR

I want to tell you something.

It's so important, I want you to listen very closely.

Ready? Listening?

We don't all agree.

Even though we are part of the same church, or the same family, or we share the same occupation or vocation, *we do not all agree.*

Oh, you realized that already?

Sometimes I get disheartened by this. Sometimes I don't know what to do with it. Sometimes I struggle with how to respond. I get discouraged by our differences, but even more so how we deal with our differences. Maybe I'm not alone in this. Maybe you've felt this too. It's not always easy.

There are so many ways to live, believe, and think.

The appropriate involvement of the government.

What we eat.

Who should be in the ministry.

Immigration.

Sexuality.

Parenting.

Yes, we are the family of God. *One family.* Yet how can we be so different? God calls us children, and other believers become our brothers and sisters—the church becomes our spiritual family. In the church, we are all brothers or sisters, mothers or fathers in the faith to those around us. We are a large, multicultural, multigenerational family of faith. But we are so different.

An Effort to Control

Throughout history, humans have made efforts to control and limit who is invited to be a disciple and become involved with God's work. The list of qualifications changed depending on the prevailing culture and involved exclusion on the basis of gender, class, race, and education.

The situation in the time of Jesus reflected this age-old human challenge. There were defined ideas of who was allowed to participate with God's work and who was not. Who had first entrance into God's presence and who was confined to the outer limits of interaction with God. In this environment, the actions of Jesus are quite surprising.

Perhaps the shock of Jesus' actions are lost on us who live in a different cultural context. Jesus called the *undesirables*, those whom others had decided were not permitted to join the work of God, to come along and join the kingdom work. This showcases that all are God's children and all are invited to follow. Inclusiveness was a core principle in the life of Jesus because this reflected the nature of God within the cultural confines of where Jesus lived. Included in this list of outsiders were:

- women (Luke 10:38-42; 8:1-3; Matthew 27:55)
- foreigners (Mark 5:1-20; Matthew 4:25)
- sinners (Matthew 9:10-13)
- tax collectors (Mark 2:13-17)
- Samaritans (John 4:1-42; Luke 10:25-37)

These groups of people that were formerly excluded were now included in the mission of Jesus Christ.

All are called to be disciples of God. Those who are black or white, Asian or Hispanic, male or female, gay or straight, rich, poor, or middle class, conservative or progressive. When I say all are called to be disciples, I mean all people. Because the gospel is for all people and meant to move each of us to faithfulness.

A large curtain separated the Holy Place from the Holy of Holies—the innermost Temple chamber that represented God's presence among the people. If you remember, when Jesus died, this was miraculously torn in two, from top to bottom, declaring that the way of approach to God was no longer found inside this granite and marble structure, but was now open to all who would enter by the sacrifice once for all given by Jesus Christ (Matthew 27:51). The new dwelling place of God is each individual who accepts this sacrifice on their behalf, is filled with the Holy Spirit, and becomes a temple of God, showcasing the glory of God in their lives.

During Jesus' final words of instruction to the 12 disciples, He commanded them to make disciples of all nations (Matthew 28:18-20). In an imperative command, Jesus said, "Go and make disciples of all nations." Jesus did not leave room for them to decide who was chosen, but instead directed them to go, and specifically told them to go everywhere—to all nations and all peoples. The phrase *all nations* knows no borders of country, language, race, or gender. For the disciples of Jesus, raised as God-fearing Jews, these orders stood in direct opposition to what they were taught and what was culturally acceptable.

After Jesus' ascension into heaven and days of prayer in the upper room in Jerusalem, the Holy Spirit was poured out onto the disciples and they began to speak in many languages (Acts 2:1-4). Peter addressed the confused crowd and quoted from the prophet Joel, linking the outpouring of the Holy Spirit with a special act of God during the last days. This outpouring of the Holy Spirit will be on all people—sons and daughters, men and women, young and old (Acts 2:17-21). Peter recognized that this was the beginning of the inclusive priesthood of all believers that Jesus' ministry inaugurated (1 Peter 2:9, 10).

A biblical theology of the call to discipleship recognizes that individuals become disciples from the first moment they accept Jesus' invitation to follow. Disciples are declared clean by Jesus—even as they are being made clean (John 8:11). This is in direct contrast with the idea of some that the individual has to get things together to be useful to God. We say "yes" in response to the love and grace of God, who always makes the first move towards us. As we journey with God, we are transformed.

The call to discipleship is an inclusive call, extended personally by God to every human being. In spite of the ways humans try to exclude one another, Jesus personally invites each one to follow God. Jesus' disciples are to reflect this same inclusion in the way they disciple diverse people groups. This same all-embracing call should pervade the current practice of discipleship, for in Jesus, all of the walls that divided and separated peoples are now torn down (Ephesians 2:14).

The Church as a Body

In Romans 12:3-8, Paul illustrates his point that the Christian community is a diverse but united whole by comparing it to a body. The imagery of the human body wasn't first used by Paul. A number of ancient writers used that metaphor for the political state—even though it was made up of many people, it made one single "body." A few writers even said that the state is the "body" of the emperor.

Paul was using the language available at the time, but scholars also see from his letter here and to the Corinthians, that this imagery of the body had deep roots in his own theology. In 1 Corinthians where Paul described how we are to take communion, he compared the body of Christ—our Savior—to the body of Christ—the church. I believe this helps us to see that Paul was thinking of Christ's death on the cross as the means by which the community came to be a community—the living body of Christ. Each of us participates equally in the benefits and gifts of Christ's redemptive work.

The church as a body is a metaphor that keeps us grounded. The church as a body is Christ manifested here in this place.

We are inescapably joined to the other members of the Christian community. We can no more separate ourselves from the body than the hand can decide it doesn't want to be attached to the arm anymore or the arm can feel it doesn't need the torso.

This is ultimately what Paul was claiming. The believers are *in Christ* and they are joined to His body, becoming His living body in the world (1 John 4:16-21; Ephesians 1:22-23).

The Church as Family

I opened this chapter by calling us a diverse, multicultural family of faith. Family imagery in the New Testament is frequent, especially in the writings of Paul. We are all adopted as children of God which unites us into one family of God (Romans 8:14-17; Ephesians 1:3-5; 1 John 3:1-2; Ephesians 3:14-19). The family is where we are nurtured and loved—where we find our place and belonging; where we feel safe to grow and stretch, becoming who we are. There's also a dark side to family. The family is the place that you experience your greatest pain and where we are most deeply wounded.[1] The church, as well as the family we are raised by, are both a place of belonging and a place of wounding. The church is called to be a part of the healing of each member of the body. For many, healing begins by knowing they are invited, knowing God welcomes them and intends them to be a disciple.

God calls us to be a healthy family. Healthy families deal with differences with humility, respect, and sensitivity. Healthy families build bridges to one another. Healthy families recognize the way each one belongs and the uniqueness of what each one brings to the family unit.

We are bonded as the people of God who are rescued by the gift of Jesus Christ. All of us. Salvation through grace alone. After all, we are only able to bridge to one another because God first bridged to each one of us (1 John 4:19). The role of the family of God is to extend the invitation to all (Matthew 24:14).

We are so diverse that we disagree and fight, yet remain in fellowship with each other anyway because of and enabled by the grace of God in our lives (1 Peter 4:8).

Next Generations

I believe one of the main things that stops us from successfully sharing our faith with next generations is this question of our welcome and how we deal with our differences.

How we welcome diversity and how we deal with our differences have great implications for our relationships, as well as the mission of the church to disciple all people. Many of us have given in to the temptation of writing people off or cutting people out who are different from us or disagree with us. If you've got people in your church, your family, or your friend group who don't agree with you (and I hope you do!), this understanding of how we can hold space for diversity can make all the difference.

Jesus started off His work here with a homogenous group. Think about it. Twelve Jewish men from a similar region of the world. Even with their differences, they had many commonalities including culture, customs, diet, religious upbringing, and family structure. Jesus started with this group that was, in many ways, very similar.

Then, in the book of Acts, we see that everything started changing. In Acts 2, we read about how thousands of believers were added to the group from all different parts of the world. But at least all were adherents to Judaism. They had a common Jewish faith they had embraced. Shortly after that, we read in Acts 10 that other Gentiles started joining in and following Jesus. Now that's when things really started to get messy!

Why did Jesus do this? Why was this part of God's plan?

Do you think the disciples were wondering that too? Jesus didn't solve it for them. He didn't give them point-by-point instructions on what to do when they disagreed. Jesus trusted His followers. There was something sacred in the mess of figuring it out together and trusting the working of the Holy Spirit. One thing I know is that it wasn't easy, but it all came together as everyone had a seat at the table.

Coming to the Table

At the first church council in Jerusalem, we see concession and compassion for one another exhibited between the Jewish and Gentile believers in the early church (Acts 15). God led the church through:

- sharing experiences of the Holy Spirit's work (Peter, Paul/Barnabas),
- exegesis of the Scriptures (James), and
- the generous character of Christian leaders (Peter, James, Paul, and Barnabas).

You see, God was leading them to a new place. It was not the same as the Jews had experienced before, and it wasn't the same as the Gentiles had experienced before. Ellen White says it this way, "We must not think, 'Well, we have all the truth, we understand the main pillars of our faith, and we may rest on this knowledge.' The truth is an advancing truth, and we must walk in the increasing light."[2] What Christ was doing with this family of God was leading them step by step, building a bridge between them. As they met on this bridge of grace, both could exclaim, "We are saved by grace 'just as they are.'"

Most of the agreements that came out of the council had to do with dietary choices because of how important table fellowship was to the early church. The church remained together, building bridges to one another, at the table. They came to the table spread by the One who first came to us.

The challenge with the spread of the gospel is that it's tempting to make new disciples just like us. If they just became like us—other cultures, people groups, next generations—it would ease the tension. If you could just believe and act the same as I do, then we can get along.

Like the early church, we must set boundaries around what is foundational—"not making it difficult" for those behind us and around us who are turning to God. We are called to build fellowship, realizing this requires sensitivity to the needs of new disciples who may think, feel, and behave differently than we do.

All Are Called to Transformation

All are called to be disciples. Fortunately for all of us, God doesn't just see who we are. God sees who we can be. God doesn't see the church as she is. God sees who she can be.

All are invited. We are a community, not defined by our collective problems, but by our creation in the image of God. Our belonging is to the One who called each one of us. Our becoming is a process. In 2 Corinthians 3:12-18, it says, "we are being transformed." The present tense indicative is used here, indicating that the action is both fully complete, yet ongoing. We experience this in the present as transformation. Yet, God continues in the ongoing work of transforming our lives day by day. Transformation is a Holy Spirit process that is both completed and "not yet."

In the church, we are known, not by what is wrong with us, but by who we are becoming. That is the gift of the church family. All are welcome. Each of us belongs. We live by God's grace—the free and unmerited favor of God—not based on what we offer to God, but what is gifted to us. This grace characterizes our day-by-day living. We recognize that none of us is finished. At the core, the life of a disciple is a life of belonging and growth. We are life-long learners seeking to be stronger and more ready to embrace the adventure of following God, as well as embracing the others who are on this shared journey together.

May you recognize that you are invited and welcomed into full belonging in the family of God.

May you experience God making space in your heart for those different from you.

May the grace of God bring understanding as we come to the table with one another.

Discussion Questions.

1. Have you or someone you know ever been excluded from discipleship or ministry? What was that experience like?
2. What does it look like today to follow the example of the church council seen in Acts 15, both in setting boundaries and "in not making it difficult" for new believers?
3. What is one action you can take this week to make space in your life for someone different from you?

CHAPTER FIVE

Bringing the Pieces Together

"The reason why many are still troubled, still seeking, still making little forward progress is because they haven't yet come to the end of themselves. We're still trying to give orders, and interfering with God's work within us."

A. W. TOZER

DR. ALLAN WALSHE TURNED TO HIS CLASS and asked a question. "On the continuum of relationship and information, with relationship being a number 1 and information being a number 10, where do you think the Adventist Church falls in its emphasis?" Most people say eight or nine; one person in the room calls out three. In the years since, I have asked this question to countless groups and the response has always been the same—a recognition that as a church we place a heavy emphasis on information, many times eclipsing the importance of a relationship with God.

In previous chapters, we have recognized that the call to "go and make disciples" goes beyond the mere transmission of information about God. Our call is to invest time relationally with others, to learn experientially how to follow God in our everyday lives. In the last chapter, we recognized that those who are invited to be disciples may not always be the ones we would choose. Still, we need each other in this process of becoming who God has called each of us to be. Discipleship is always found in the context of community.

It would be natural to focus on a curriculum that prioritizes right information about discipleship as if to say, "If you know these things about a relationship with Jesus, prayer, and devotional time in the Word of God, then you will have growth in the life of the disciple." From the study of Scripture and from experience, I have come to realize that it's not information *or* relationship, but information in the context of relationship. We need both in order to experience growth. Yet, the order is important. Information and learning must come in a relationship and experience with a personal God. The journey in community and the focus on experiential learning that are inherent in discipleship allow us to maintain a focus on both relationship and right information (life-giving truth) at the same time.

Biblical Foundations of a Discipleship Journey

Christ's appeal to the church from the Scriptures is to move beyond lukewarm religion into an authentic discipleship relationship (Revelation 3:14-20). A discipleship journey can support this momentum towards an authentic relationship. The following principles, from our study in this and the previous chapters, serve as the biblical foundation for the discipleship journey shared in this book.

1. Discipleship centers on Jesus Christ and following Christ as the foundation of all religious belief and practice (Galatians 6:14). As everything in the church and the created world is held together in Christ, so God, as revealed in Jesus, must remain the center of discipleship—all of our belief and practice (Colossians 1:15-20).

2. Discipleship is personal—characterized by a personal call from God —"Come follow me" (Matthew 4:19; Mark 1:17).

3. Discipleship is relational—a friendship with God —"He appointed twelve that they might *be with him* and that he might send them out to preach" (Mark 3:14, emphasis added). Scripture affirms that God's desire is to be near the church, sharing an intimate relationship with God's people (James 4:8; John 15:15; Revelation 3:20; Romans 8:15).

4. Discipleship is demanding—costing everything—"Whoever wants to be my disciple must deny themselves and take up their cross daily and follow me" (Luke 9:23). Jesus must be Lord in the disciple's life, regardless of what persecution, challenge, or rejection may follow.

5. Discipleship must take place in the context of community—love for one another bears witness to Jesus—"Therefore encourage one another and build each other up" (1 Thessalonians 5:11). The call to discipleship cannot be separated from a call to become a part of the body of Christ (1 Corinthians 12:12-14) for it is through the body that disciples understand what it looks like to follow Jesus. Paul instructed believers to imitate his example (1 Corinthians 4:16), as well as the example of God in Jesus Christ (Ephesians 5:1-2).

6. Discipleship is missional—following Jesus in His mission in the world—"I will make you fishers of people" (Matthew 4:19; Mark 1:17). While the call is a personal one to be with Jesus, it is also imperative to be with Jesus where He goes—on a mission to reach and to save the world.

7. Discipleship is inclusive of all people regardless of race, gender, or age—"Go and make disciples of all nations" (Matthew 28:19-20). Especially in the last days, the Holy Spirit will use all parts of the body of Christ to proclaim the Good News and invite others to find salvation in Christ (Acts 2:17-21).

The *Deep Calling* discipleship journey is built on these foundational principles. This foundation serves as a catalyst for genuine growth in the life of the believer. This growth is experienced in three overlapping and interrelated areas: deeper devotion to God, richer life in community, and greater purpose in mission.

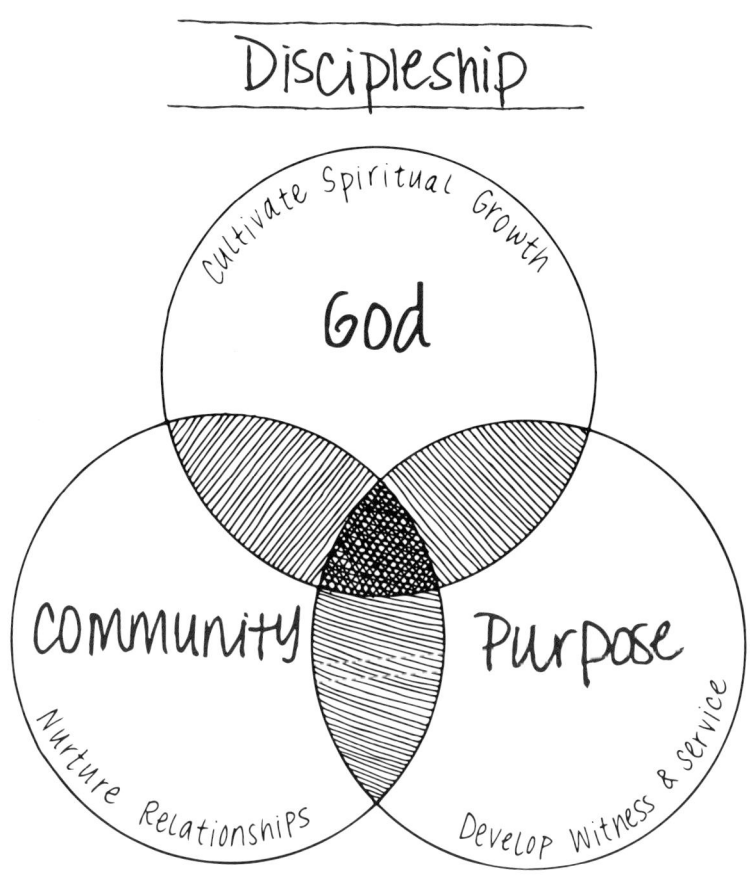

Deepening Experience with GOD

Following Jesus is a costly venture. It requires everything. Peter declared, "We have left everything to follow you!" (Mark 10:28). Jesus replied, "No one who has left home or brothers or sisters or mother or father or children or fields for me and the gospel will fail to receive a hundred times as much in this present age: homes, brothers, sisters, mothers, children and fields—along with persecutions—and in the age to come eternal life" (Mark 10:29-31). Being a disciple of Jesus demands all, comes with persecution, and is at the same time richly rewarding in both the present life and the life to come (John 10:10; Psalm 16:11; Isaiah 35:10).

The cost of discipleship is described in Luke 14:25-33. In verse 27, Jesus said, "Whoever does not carry their cross and follow me cannot be my disciple." In verse 33, He reiterated, "In the same way, those of you who do not give up everything you have cannot be my disciples." Jesus then went on to caution the disciples to count the cost before deciding to follow, for it would cost them everything (Matthew 19:23-30). The call to become a disciple of Jesus is more than accepting Christ as Savior; It is the devotion of the entire life to God's will and purposes. This is how disciples grow deeper in their experience with God.

What does this look like today? This means a complete surrender of my life—not only my time, resources, and gifts, but also my hopes, desires, and longings. It means reorienting my priorities to live in faithfulness to God's call. It means laying down my concern for the opinions of others. Understanding the costly nature of discipleship reframes the suffering I've been through and the stillborn dreams I have experienced in my life.

A disciple's sacrifices reveal the value they place on following Jesus. Like the person who found a pearl of great price and sold all they had to obtain it (Matthew 13:45-46), so is the person who forsakes all other priorities to follow Jesus, for they have found God to be worth more than anything else.

Ellen White asserted that discipleship is seen in the everyday actions of the believer:

> True religion means living the word in your practical life. Your profession is not of any value without the practical doing of the word. "If any man will come after Me, let him deny himself, and take up his cross daily, and follow Me." This is the condition of discipleship.[1]

As disciples practice faith in day-to-day life, they experience what it means to take up their cross and follow. It is through this surrender that we experience growth in God.

The call to be a disciple is both personal and relational. Jesus calls each individual by name and invites them to experience a living, daily relationship with God. In response to this call, it becomes the paramount need of the disciple to focus on Jesus as the center of life and the spiritual journey. This calling is costly, for accepting the Lordship of Jesus displaces all the other lords in the life of the disciple. Yet, the disciple has found Jesus to be worth giving up anything for. This is the heart of discipleship. Suffering and surrender cultivate spiritual growth in the believer through a deepening experience of relationship with God.

Deepening Relationships in Community

A remarkable sense of community develops among disciples who are following Jesus together in mission. What binds the community of disciples together? First, as Dietrich Bonhoeffer points out, each disciple has experienced the forgiveness of sins in Jesus Christ.[2] It is this understanding of who disciples were before encountering Jesus, and who they are now in Jesus that characterizes the relationships between believers. All those gathered to Jesus know that without God, they are without hope. Together they stand on common ground as they recognize that they are sinners saved by grace

(Ephesians 2:4-6; 1 Peter 2:9). Second, it is the shared commission to do Jesus' work in the world that unifies God's people together (Matt 28:18-20). God lives in the church (Ephesians 2:19-22) and is reconciling the world through God's people (2 Corinthians 5:17-21). This binds believers even more closely together as the body of Christ (1 Corinthians 12).

For disciples, the life, death, and resurrection of Jesus changes how they interact with others. Notice that after Pentecost, the group of original disciples allowed Jesus to form their lives around their relationships with God and the people around them. Acts 2:46-47 describes this: "Every day they continued to meet together in the temple courts. They broke bread in their homes and ate together with glad and sincere hearts, praising God and enjoying the favor of all the people. And the Lord added to their number daily those who were being saved." As they were united together with Jesus and each other, God was able to continue to add people to the church. Church growth is spoken of in relational terms—between God and the believer, as well as among the believers themselves. As the church met, ate, praised, and enjoyed favor together, God was able to bring about growth. **The community they experienced led to expansion.**

This does not mean that community comes easily or quickly. Genuine community comes about as people follow Christ together, and it is not something that humans can fabricate themselves. Not unlike the salvation experience, community is a gift that only God can give.[3] It is God who drives all aspects of authentic Christian community. The disciple's ongoing experience with Jesus' extravagant forgiveness slowly transforms them into a person who forgives others (Ephesians 4:31-32). The disciple's experience with God's consistent love changes them into a person who shares love with others (1 Corinthians 13:4-7). The way the disciple treats others is evidence of God's work in them. The outward fruit testifies to the inward transformation (Luke 6:43-45).

Why will spiritual transformation through an emphasis on discipleship make a more vibrant church culture? Disciples who have a living relationship with Jesus through which they are experiencing God's love, mercy, and joy, bear the same fruit in their relationships with others. For example, many of the spiritual disciplines are centered around listening to God. By learning to listen to God, disciples learn to listen to those around them—both in and outside of the church. By listening more deeply to those around them, they are better able to reach them with the good news of Jesus and God's love for them. In communicating the love of Christ, the disciple is accomplishing the mission.

It is the expression of Jesus' love in the life of the community that works to draw others into a relationship with God (John 17:20-23). Jesus said that it is by love expressed to one another that people would be able to recognize His disciples (John 13:34-35). This was true then, and it is true now.

It is the love of Jesus that binds disciples together and prepares them for their work with Jesus in the world. Ellen White shares the winsome nature of this love in the following way:

> The knowledge of the Saviour's matchless love for them (the disciples) was to bind them heart to heart, preparing the way for the Lord to anoint them with his Spirit. United by this love, they were to go forth to witness with convincing power to the divinity of their Leader. And their Christlike love for one another was to be the sign of their discipleship.[4]

The Savior's love, unity in the church, and power in witnessing are all realized in the lives of the believers as they follow Jesus together on mission in the world. Out of this fusion comes the divine gift of community and sense of belonging for the believers.

Disciples are established in Christ individually, but there is an aspect of the love of Christ that is not able to be realized outside of the community of faith. Only together with all the saints are disciples able to grasp how wide, long, high, and deep is Christ's love (Ephesians 3:17b-19). There is a richer understanding of Jesus that is understood within the body of Christ. Community is essential to the formation of the follower of Jesus.

A Deepening Experience of Purpose

The invitation to be with Jesus as His disciple is inseparable from the invitation to follow Christ on mission in the world (Mark 1:17-18; 3:14). In the Scriptures, discipleship and mission are an integrated calling lived out in the day-to-day experience through witness and service.

In 2 Corinthians 5:17-21, Paul succinctly summarizes the interconnectedness of becoming a disciple and heeding the call to mission. He asserts that believers are reconciled to Christ, made into new creations, and given the ministry of reconciliation. These three truths, which are often compartmentalized in church processes, are actually inseparably bound together in the Scriptures.

Believers' sins are not counted against them (justification) as they experience God's reconciliation and recreative power (sanctification), which enables them and compels them to share the good news of these realities (evangelism). The disciple is called to appeal to others to experience what they are experiencing. This is the calling of every believer, not just a select few. The only qualification for belonging to the priesthood of all believers as spoken of in 1 Peter 2:9 is the experience of being called "out of darkness into his wonderful light." All who are called out of darkness by Jesus are likewise called to live out the mission of Jesus through the Holy Spirit.

God desires for salvation to reach the ends of the earth—to every person, tribe, and nation—not just the people of Israel. Even before His coming, it was foretold of Jesus, "It is too small a thing that You should be My Servant to raise up the tribes of Jacob and to restore the preserved ones of Israel; I will also make You a light of the nations so that My salvation may reach to the end of the earth" (Isaiah 49:6, NASB). The scope of the mission of Christ is immense. Christ came to earth with the mission to save the entire world (John 3:16, 17). Jesus gave life more abundantly through the sacrifice of His life (John 10:10). How did Jesus choose to live out this mission to save the world? Jesus chose to call disciples.

As Jesus walked beside the Sea of Galilee, He saw Peter and Andrew fishing. Mark 1:17-18 recounts, "'Come, follow me,' Jesus said, 'and I will send you out to fish for people.' At once they left their nets and followed him." The disciples were invited to participate in the redemptive work of God in the world, through Jesus Christ. As they were learning to follow Jesus and how to imitate Him, Jesus had them practice what He taught them and took time to process their learning and growth (Luke 10:1-20). As a result of their time with Jesus, Jesus' love for the world gradually became internalized in the life of the disciples. Jesus sent them into the world to be among the people just as Jesus had been among them (John 17:18).

The call to be a disciple is by nature missional, for the disciple is invited to follow after Jesus in mission to the world. As disciples spend time in Jesus' Presence, the love of Christ for the world becomes a part of them. The disciple, in turn, then lives out this love in the world through witness and service. This mission is fulfilled in the context of community, while growth through relationship with God in surrender and suffering is taking place in the life of the believer.

The Future

It's my prayer that in future years the Adventist Church will more wholly embrace a relational focus of discipleship. When a group of Adventists are asked this question in the future, "On the continuum of Relationship and Information, with relationship being number 1 and information being number 10, where do you think the Adventist Church falls in its emphasis?" the answer will indicate that we firmly prioritize the importance of a relationship with God for every believer.

> *May you know the delight of joining God in the mission of sharing love to the world.*
>
> *May you understand both the sacrificial cost and joy of discipleship.*
>
> *May you experience the messy, but Divine gift of community with other believers.*

Discussion Questions

1. In what way has personally experiencing the love of Jesus impacted how you view the mission of Jesus?
2. What is one of the most significant sacrifices you've made in following Christ as His disciple? What is one of the richest joys?
3. What is an area of slow, difficult community-building that your church faces right now? How can you encourage them?

CHAPTER SIX

What's Bothering You?

"When Jesus said, 'Come to me, all you who labor and are heavy burdened,' He assumed we would grow weary, discouraged, and disheartened along the way. These words are a touching testimony to the genuine humanness of Jesus. He had no romantic notion of the cost of discipleship. He knew that following Him was as unsentimental as duty, as demanding as love."

BRENNAN MANNING

DALLAS WILLARD INSISTS that instead of trying to think of what you are passionate about and where you feel called to invest, answer a different question. His question arrested my attention and has been a reorienting call over the years:

What's bothering you?[1]

What's bothering you can lead you to the very area where you are called to make a difference.

This is exactly how it worked for one of my heroes, Mister Rogers. In an interview with CNN in 1999, he said, "I went into television because I hated it so. And I thought, there's some way of using this fabulous instrument to nurture those who would watch and listen."[2]

There has to be a way…

Perhaps, like me, you find yourself able to make a long list of what is bothering you. In the context of the church, several things have troubled me, bothering me to the point that I found myself thinking, "There has to be a way."

- Treasuring our special knowledge while at the same time living in insecurity about our salvation.
- Thinking it can't be a call from God unless it is outside your gifts and passions.
- The idea that spiritual life and growth look the same for every believer.
- Believing there are some who are "spiritual" and some who are not; some who can pray and some who can't.
- "Once I came into the truth…" – as if truth is a destination we arrive at.
- Counting some people out of Divine favor.

These are just some of the things on my list. There has to be a way, I thought, to allow people space to experience God, develop security in God's love, to be set free to live their unique purpose, and come to the realization that this is a lifelong journey.

With the majority of Seventh-day Adventist churches in North America in a state of plateau or decline, the question must be asked: Do we have a discipleship strategy that is working?

In 20 years of ministry, I can see that the discipleship principles have been at work in my ministry from the beginning. The things that were most meaningful and fulfilling always took place when I joined Jesus in the work of being and making disciples. In the last 10 years, though, I have been led to prioritize the invitation of Jesus to make disciples in an even more intentional way. First and foremost, I've been making more space in my life to be a disciple of Jesus (Matthew 28:18-20). Second, this inward journey has led me to invite others to participate in an intentional discipleship process and respond to the eight calls of God in the context of community. I try to guard this time to share my personal experience with others in the ongoing discipleship process, but ever present is the opportunity to be distracted.

    I believe there is nothing more important than prioritizing (1) being a disciple and (2) joining God in making disciples. I believe this is true. You might even agree with me. Yet, how do we see this reflected in our schedules? In the way we pull back to sit in the presence of God? In our teaching and preaching? God continues to invite me into this way of life—this sacred priority of being and growing disciples.

    What distracts us from this focus on discipleship? We have the regular distractions that anyone has—a finite amount of time, the pressure of too much to do, and the external expectations of others on our time and attention, to name a few. Beyond these common struggles, Seventh-day Adventists struggle with unique distractions from discipleship.

    For some Seventh-day Adventists, the focus placed on *right* beliefs has overshadowed the importance of spiritual development and transformation brought about by a relationship with Christ and the presence of the Holy Spirit (see 2 Corinthians 3:18; Galatians 5:22-25; Ezekiel 37:1-14; Romans 12:2). We are able to *believe* all the right things, and yet remain unchanged in our spiritual life. Many times, we are so focused on having *the truth* that we forget that, as disciples, we are following the *Truth* in the person of Jesus Christ. This failure to experience a vibrant relationship with Christ in turn arrests involvement in the missional and evangelistic ministry of Christ (see Matthew 28:19-20; Luke 4:15-21).

The church has taught people doctrinal theology (how to believe), but has neglected to teach them moral theology and ethics (how to behave in society) and devotional theology (how to relate spiritually to God and others).[3] The abandonment of teaching these three elements of theology, and the exclusive emphasis on the one element, doctrinal theology, has left many Seventh-day Adventists longing for more.

Church members can have orthodox Adventist beliefs, yet remain unchanged in their heart and lifestyle. Being an Adventist Christian does not make them any more loving, joyful, kind, or long-suffering (Galatians 5:22-23) than they were before they joined the church. As Russell Burrill states, "They know the truth, but do not know the *Truth*."[4] For some members, belief in Jesus seems to be a transaction which brings salvation, getting them into heaven someday, but does not develop into a living relationship. Sadly, for some it doesn't even give assurance and peace in their own spiritual journey.

Still for others, Jesus is *one* of their doctrines, but not *the One* who is the foundation of all other doctrines and beliefs (Colossians 1:16-17). The church has been unsuccessful in leading them to see that a relationship with Jesus, learning how to follow Him, is *the* central point of their faith.

In Jesus' final address to His disciples, He commanded them to "make disciples of all nations (Matthew 28:19-20). Yet, we are so often distracted from being and growing disciples. We easily get caught up in other things we are doing as a church. Although there are many distractions that could be highlighted, I believe there are three that deserve our focus – three primary behavior patterns which distract us from prioritizing discipleship in the Seventh-day Adventist Church: legalism, compartmentalization, and fear of deception.

Legalism

Legalism is a warped understanding that humans can control their own transformation, experiencing this change by their strength alone. Legalists have bought into the hope that they will be able to alter their behaviors to be in alignment with the life of Christ. Instead of a position of trust in Jesus, the focus shifts from God to the person as they try to *do it right*. Relying upon Jesus and the work He is doing is uncomfortable and lengthy. In a church with high moral and behavioral standards, such as the Seventh-day Adventist Church, it is easy for members to focus on their conduct as an indicator of their relationship to God. Sabbath observance, diet, dress, and acts of service become proof of acceptance by God. As attention is fixed on external behavior, the believer is drawn away from the life-transforming inner relationship with Jesus. When challenges are encountered, believers can find themselves asking, "What was I doing wrong?" in order for this to happen.

Compartmentalization

Compartmentalization occurs when believers view their spirituality as one facet of life, rather than as a radical shift that transforms the entire life. As with legalism, Jesus is not Lord; the individual is. Without examples in the body of Christ and relationships that show how to be disciples—coaching, practice, and peer-to-peer mentoring—many believers continue to live out the same routines they have always had. The only difference is that they come to church on Saturdays. Their primary understanding and identification is not as a disciple of Jesus, but as a member of the church. Faith does not affect the rest of their lives—their Monday-through-Friday lives. An intentional discipleship process is essential for each local church to train people in how to surrender to Jesus and experience transforming power daily.

Before moving on to the third distraction, it is important

to acknowledge that there is tension between legalism and compartmentalization. Either striving to keep the law or working hard at the spiritual disciplines can become legalistic in approach. It's important to remain sensitive to the fact that it is possible to become legalistic in the way we approach discipleship. Jesus, not the individual, must remain the primary focus. The Christian life is primarily what is being done to you, not what you are doing.[6]

Fear of Deception

The fear of deception is a growing and prevalent distraction from discipleship in the Seventh-day Adventist Church. This fear of deception affects many aspects of the spiritual life by diverting the focus of the disciple from a relationship with Jesus to learning *truth* in order to avoid deception. Fear of deception paralyzes the disciple's pursuit of a personal relationship with Christ, and instead, prioritizes correct knowledge as the source of security. This fear results in a form of evangelism which emphasizes the transmission of right information in order to safeguard the hearers from deception.

This emphasis on avoiding deception often ends up eclipsing the necessity of having a relationship with Jesus and inviting others to follow Him. The Bible confronts this emphasis on fear and deception. The Bible declares, "Perfect love drives out all fear" (1 John 4:18), including the fear of being deceived. As believers live in a relationship with Jesus and submit to God's will, they have nothing to fear. Again, the Scriptures emphasize, "Greater is He who is in you than He who is in the world" (1 John 4:4). The Lord provides protection in Christ and in the Word of God (Ephesians 6:17). As disciples are rooted in Christ, they are able to stand against deception. Paul's counsel to the Colossians is to "continue to live in Him" (Colossians 2:6-8). Later, in his counsel to Timothy, he stated that "God has not given us a spirit of fear and timidity, but of power, love and a sound mind" (2 Timothy 1:7). Jesus is the way to security in this life (John 14:6).

Some have even feared silence and stillness with God, worried that the enemy would whisper in their mind and take over their lives. Special inspiration testifies, "When every other voice is hushed, when every earthly interest is turned aside, the silence of the soul makes more distinct the voice of God."[6]

I have talked with church members who felt so afraid of deception in the way they were praying that they took a break from prayer altogether. I am not alone in this experience. Other pastors have shared similar stories with me.

In response to our tendency towards legalism, God responds with grace.

In response to our compartmentalized life, God calls us to integration.

In response to our fear of deception, God promises to hold us in perfect peace.

What's Bothering You?

Leader, I'm wondering, what's bothering you? Is there a way discipleship is being missed in your life and in your church? Remember, this is much more than about you or me. There are some who are deeply bothered by where we are as a church right now. Some of you are despairing about where you are on your spiritual journey—you long for more. How is it that God wants to lead you from that place to nurturing new life?

This process you're embarking on is not just about you as an individual. Or about your local church. It's about all of us. As you are healthier, so we are healthier. Each of us must come alive to what God has called us to. Who are you serving? Who is this about? Let's spur one another on towards courage and hope in what God is doing among us.

It's about deepening your love and trust in God.

It's about discovering more of who you are.

It's about imagining what is not yet in our church and in our communities.

It's about making a difference by growing disciples.

It's about learning how to dream, implement, and discover.

For some, it will also be about pushing yourself to make time for what matters most. Opening up to the power of God at work in your life. Being real with others about your longing for God.

May you feel your own heart stirred to longing after God, even in the midst of distractions.

May you know God wants nothing more than for you to be a disciple and join God in making disciples.

May you join God in this sacred work of being and growing disciples by ruthlessly making space for what matters most.

Discussion Questions.

1. What's bothering you? Is there an invitation from God there?
2. Where is there the greatest need in your church: doctrinal, moral, or devotional theology? What is one way you can help balance and focus your growth as a church this week?
3. Which of the three distractions—legalism, compartmentalization, or fear of deception—have you struggled with the most? How does the discipleship process re-focus on Jesus?

CHAPTER SEVEN

Discipleship and the Adventist Church

"It is not earthly rank, nor birth, nor nationality, nor religious privilege, which proves that we are members of the family of God; it is love, a love that embraces all humanity."

ELLEN WHITE

I LOVE THE SEVENTH-DAY ADVENTIST CHURCH. Let me tell you a few reasons why.

- We are a people who believe we are accepted fully and completely by God because of grace through Jesus. The gift of righteousness given to us by Jesus changes our lives.
- We are a movement defined by a continued search for truth. As a lifelong learner, I love this about our church.
- We are people who hold on tenaciously to hope for all people. We are people of the Advent—the hope of renewal, restoration, and recreation.

- We are people who believe all individuals deserve rest, including the manservant or maidservant—which means the minimum wage worker, not just the salaried professional, deserves the human dignity of worth that comes from resting, knowing that our worth comes not from what we do, but from who we are.
- We are a people of purpose. We believe Jesus has called us to make a tangible difference in the world (Matthew 25; Luke 4:18-19) and we engage this together.
- We are a people who believe God wants to transform this world radically. God doesn't want to get rid of this earth, but wants to restore it, making the prayer "On earth as it is in heaven" our reality.

There are so many reasons, I could go on. I believe this church, this church you're a part of, this church you're leading, or perhaps this church you're currently struggling with, is beautiful. Let me acknowledge right up front that this has always been and will always be an imperfect church. Imperfect people that we are, as long as we are here, it will be imperfect. Yet, all the same, what God is doing in our midst is worthy of celebration.

Discipleship in the Adventist Church

At this point, two decades into the 21st Century, there are divergent definitions held by members of the Seventh-day Adventist Church regarding what is central to faith. The Adventist Church has a statement of 28 fundamental beliefs, which describe in detail the breadth of Adventist doctrine as drawn from the Word of God. Doctrinal formulations, by their very nature, do and should leave room for interpretation and practical application in the lives of individual members and local churches. As a result, there are many different interpretations of what it means to live a Seventh-day Adventist lifestyle.

Given these differing interpretations of doctrine in the Adventist Church, is it possible to find a uniting paradigm of discipleship? Based on the biblical study in the previous chapters, we will unpack how this can be applied specifically in the Seventh-day Adventist Church, though I believe this application extends to other contexts as well.

Three principles will be helpful in moving toward a common understanding of what is central to faith and the subsequent establishment of a process of discipleship in the church.

The Role of Scripture

First, in defining discipleship, the Bible must be maintained as the authority in determining the principles and practice of nurturing a personal relationship with God. The Bible is inspired by God (2 Peter 1:20-21) and testifies of Jesus (John 5:39). Therefore, the Word of God must guide understanding and be the authenticator of personal, heart experience. This, however, does not put the Bible in the place of Jesus, as if we were worshipping the Bible itself or the knowledge received from study, but emphasizes that it is the only source for seeking the rule of faith and practice. The written Word of God exists to lead us to the Living Word of God, Jesus Christ (John 5:37-39; Hebrews 10:1). According to 2 Timothy 3:15, the Scriptures bring understanding and knowledge, which in turn leads to salvation through faith in Jesus Christ. If we ever struggle with understanding the Bible, we are to turn to the Living Word made Flesh (John 1) and understand a clearer picture of what God is like by how Jesus lived in this world. This guides our discipleship journey.

Jesus at the Center

Second is the recognition that the Bible declares Jesus as Lord, demanding that disciples surrender all other things to this Lordship, including all beliefs and practices (Galatians 2:20,

Philippians 2:9-11, John 14:6). This emphasis on Christ does not diminish the importance of other biblical truth—for the Scriptures make it clear that *all things* are held together in Him. Rather, Jesus puts these understandings in their proper focus (Colossians 1:16-17). As Elder Dan Jackson shares, "Christ is the center and substance of our faith."[1] Jesus is the fulfillment of the law and prophets (Matthew 5:17). In Jesus, all doctrines make sense and become profitable in the life of the disciple (2 Timothy 3:15-16).

Relationship, Not Just Information

Third, in practice, not just our words, we must value the experience of a relationship *with* God, as well as information *about* God. Adventists hold in common a conviction that the Seventh-day Adventist Church was raised up to restore certain biblical understandings to the broader, Christian church. Among these are the biblical Sabbath, what happens after death, and the nature of hell fire. While emphasizing these and other distinctive beliefs, the focus on discipleship and the imperative of having a relationship with God is, at times, minimized. This living relationship with God then becomes secondary to the *distinctive* truths which the Seventh-day Adventist Church teaches from the Scriptures. Information is important, for it is through biblical teaching that individuals are able to understand who God is and what God is like. Nevertheless, information without the context of a living relationship with Jesus is dead.

What We Bring: the Adventist Contribution to Discipleship

The Seventh-day Adventist Church has much to offer in the area of discipleship and spiritual growth. Here are four contributions that I believe are significant to the process of discipleship in the local church.

Personal Devotional Habits: As a community of faith, the Adventist Church espouses core beliefs that encourage a rule of life, that elevate the importance of the Word of God, and that stress the necessity of personal prayer.[2]

Sabbath Practice: Adventists emphasize that every member experience a weekly Sabbath as God commanded,[3] a practice which Christians from many traditions are recently rediscovering.[4]

The Role of the Holy Spirit: Even more important, the Seventh-day Adventist Church emphasizes the changes that God brings in the life of a believer through the indwelling of the Holy Spirit.[5]

Wholistic Perspective: Rather than a compartmentalized faith, Adventist doctrine encourages a wholistic view of human existence, recognizing that God wants to redeem every area of life.[6]

Challenges

Amid these blessings, there are also difficulties. As a result of the emphasis on doctrine in the Adventist Church, people can feel that once they embrace new beliefs, they have "arrived." In reality, discipleship is a process that takes time and intentional openness over the course of a lifetime. In his work centering on the mission of the local Adventist Church, Russell Burrill points out that the word *disciple* "does not suggest a rapid conversion . . . but a slow process by which one is made into a disciple."[7] Discipleship must be recaptured as a process, rather than an event.[8] It is imperative that the Seventh-day Adventist Church become deliberate about this heart-focused process.

Discipling Next Generations

Young people are especially adept at noticing the emptiness of religious practice without a living relationship. They can help the Seventh-day Adventist Church gauge effectiveness in these important areas of discipleship. Studies show that approximately half of Adventist young people in North America leave the church in their twenties.[9] Researchers agree: the attrition of youth and young adults in the Seventh-day Adventist Church continues at a steady pace.[10] I believe this is because of a failure to connect them with the heart of what following God is all about: a relationship with Jesus, joining God in mission, meaningful community, while viewing suffering from a redemptive perspective.

The best indication of whether a young person stays in the church is not how well they do in Bible class, or even daily study of the quarterly (though attending an Adventist school and engaging in Sabbath School can make a positive difference). It's the relationships that they have built with loving, Seventh-day Adventist Christian adults who are willing to journey with them as they discover what it looks like to be disciples of Jesus themselves. Information matters when it is experienced in the context of a relationship. When their faith is challenged and what they thought they understood becomes irrelevant, to whom do they turn?

The Bible calls for discipling children in the way of the Lord, aiding them to stay on this path when they grow up (Proverbs 22:6). It is in everyday interactions that parents and other adults are called to disciple children, teaching them to see Christ as the one who holds all of life together (Colossians 1:16-17). The biblical mandate is to raise up faithful disciples in those who are young so that they understand what it means to follow God and to see God in all of life. While this does not guarantee that young people will make the decision to remain part of the church as they grow older, it gives them a better opportunity because they will have seen and experienced first-hand the joys of following. One of the primary challenges of discipleship in the Adventist Church is prioritizing the discipling of young people in what it means to follow Jesus day by day.

The Importance of Discipleship

Each disciple is called to follow God and to be transformed like Jesus in doctrine, behavior, purpose, and relationships. Discipleship is about the integration of the entire life of the disciple under the instruction of the Master, Jesus.[11] It is essential for the Seventh-day Adventist Church to elevate the importance of intentional discipleship.

The crisis of plateaued or declining churches could indicate that correct beliefs are not enough for people to realize spiritual growth. There must be an intentional focus on Jesus and discipleship in the local church. This, in turn, will result in transformation and mission orientation in members.[12]

We have all dealt with our share of struggle. Disharmony, chaos, darkness, pain. This is the Great Controversy. Yet, Adventists believe harmony is coming. Love, unity, completion, renewal, and wholeness are our story. God comes to show the way. Adventists believe that living in light and life start now through a relationship with God, the One who loves us deeply and completely. Relationship. It's what changes our lives.

The In-Between

We live in between the inauguration and the consummation of the new covenant. Discipleship is the ongoing transformation of the people God is creating in the midst of the sinful, messy, and beautiful world, showing the power of the Spirit hovering over our lives. The display of God's righteousness and glory is seen in both the work of redemption and transformation, as well as the final restoration into the image of Christ when He comes.

"We have this treasure in earthen vessels, that the surpassing power may be seen of God and not of ourselves" (2 Corinthians 4:6-7). In God, we not only find forgiveness, grace, and a call to be disciples ourselves, but we find transformation in the way we treat other people and invite them to be disciples too.

The Remnant

Seventh-day Adventists believe in a faithful group of followers who are on earth at the close of history. What characteristics mark this remnant? The remnant are a people called out for the sake of the world. Not an organization unto themselves, but a people faithful to God, in order to draw other people into faithfulness to God (see Exodus 32). Blessed with a precious relationship with God so that they can be a blessing to others, inviting them into relationship. According to Revelation, these people keep the commandments—they live in the way God designed—and have a testimony or experience with Jesus themselves. The people described are disciples—following after Jesus and living the way He lived, while experiencing Jesus and sharing their testimony of that experience (Revelation 14:12). This is discipleship. This is the call of the remnant.

The Call to Sacrifice

Captain Lawrence Chambers was in the first month of his command of the USS Enterprise. He was the first African American in history to command a US Navy aircraft carrier. It was early April of 1975 and the Vietnam War was coming to an end. The United States was engaged in operation "Frequent Wind," which meant the Navy was evacuating all remaining US nationals and as many South Vietnamese military personnel and their families as possible in order to protect them from almost certain death at the hands of the North Vietnamese army as it pushed southward. The Enterprise was fully loaded with helicopters for the evacuation and had received thousands of grateful evacuees. The last helicopters were arriving when the officers on the bridge of the Enterprise received word that a small fixed wing aircraft was slowly approaching. They attempted to contact the unidentified craft on all frequencies but received only static.

A few hours earlier, a young South Vietnamese military officer realized that he and family were not going to make it out before the enemy troops arrived to kill them. Fortunately, Major Buang Lee was an experienced pilot. He sneaked onto the airbase with his family and crammed his wife and five children into a tiny two-seater Cessna O-1 training plane. They took off amid gunfire and somehow made it out over the sea. He had no idea where they would go to survive. Suddenly he spotted the cluster of ships making up Operation Frequent Wind. The plane's radio was broken.

As the officers on the Enterprise tried to identify this strange plane's intentions, they noticed, through their binoculars, children looking out of the cockpit windows. The plane circled and the pilot kept throwing papers out which kept blowing away in the wind. He finally wrapped a note around his service pistol and threw it out. It read:

> "Can you move the Helicopter to the side, I can land on your runway, I can fly 1 hour more, Please rescue me.
> - Major Buang, wife and 5 child."[13]

The officers of the Enterprise held an emergency meeting. The ship's main power plant was down for maintenance, leaving them with little power for maneuvering. The flight deck was covered with chained down Huey Helicopters that had been used in the evacuation. Captain Chambers and his team felt certain that the family had little chance of survival if they ditched in the cold South China sea. They needed to land on the Enterprise. The crew immediately put all ship systems on emergency generator power as the main power plant was put back in operation. All hands were called to the flight deck, where they were ordered to start stripping gear from the helicopters and began pushing them over the edge of the flight deck and into the sea. Working together, the crew picked up over 10 million dollars' worth of helicopters with their bare hands, and threw them into the ocean. As the crew worked to clear a space, five more helicopters arrived – they were quickly unloaded and then pitched into the sea as well.

With only minutes of fuel remaining, Major Buang brought his tiny craft in for a perfect landing on the deck of the Enterprise. He and his family were greeted with cheers and waving open arms. The crew unanimously donated money toward a fund to help the Lee family settle in the United States after claiming refugee status. Chambers was certain that his decision would get him a court martial and end his career. Thankfully his decision was upheld by his superiors, and he went on to become a Rear Admiral.

Captain Chambers chose compassion. In the split second he had to make a decision to save a family, he put their lives above his own, knowing this could be the end of his career, a career he had worked so hard for. Yet, he chose to save lives and worked with an entire crew, who together made space and saved an entire family, those precious seven people.

As disciples, we realize there's so much we cannot control. We cannot control what happens to us or what happens in the world. We cannot control what happens in our cities or in the lives of our members, but we can put ourselves in a position to experience God's transformation. To grow as disciples, being transformed to embrace the world. We can open ourselves up to bring life to the lives of others. Captain Chambers did whatever it took to bring life to the family. He was willing to let go of precious things, costly things that got in the way of making space for those individuals running on empty. The remnant are called to make space for others too. They are to bring life, salvation and healing from God. The faithful people of God experience God themselves and then relentlessly focus on being used by God to disciple others.

To be the remnant means we are transformed to love others as God loves them. We are willing to work together to do whatever it takes to be disciples and to grow other disciples.

When we started as a Seventh-day Adventist Church, there was risk and bravery and courage. There was faithfulness as our founders stepped into the territory where God was leading with very few guarantees. It was not certain, neat, or packaged into a set of fundamental beliefs, but our founders said, we will follow where God leads us.

This means that even now, in this new territory in our time and place, "we have nothing to fear for the future, except as we shall forget the way the Lord has led us, and His teaching in our past history."[14] We don't need to fear. God's presence is with us and the Present Truth will be available to us for what we face today.

May you see the beauty and the gift of being a part of the diverse, imperfect body of Christ.

May you recognize the great value God places on each person - you and everyone you meet.

May you commit your life and ministry to doing whatever it takes to be a disciple and grow other disciples, even at great sacrifice.

Discussion Questions.

1. What is one thing you love about the Adventist church?
2. Which of the four Adventist contributions to discipleship is most needed by the world? Your church? You?
3. Thinking of the story of Captain Chambers, what helicopters in the church or in your life do you believe are worth throwing overboard to make space for people in need?

CHAPTER EIGHT

Foundational Values of Discipleship

"The life of faith is represented as receiving—an act which implies the very opposite of anything like merit. It is simply the acceptance of a gift."

CHARLES SPURGEON

I AM GATHERING MY THINGS TO GET UP TO PREACH when I feel something slipping out of my Bible and I reach to grasp it. Seeing it brings a smile to my face.

It's a magnet. A small alien, complete with an extra-large head and characteristic neon green color. My colleague and friend gave it to me and I keep it in my Bible to help me remember my calling to preach a living Word each week. A strange symbol perhaps, but a meaningful one. It's easy to get knowledge-heavy. To get up front and preach or teach focused on what we want people to know and understand. Yet, we don't want to grow "aliens"—people with heads swollen up with facts alone. We want to grow disciples. We want wholistic, grounded disciples of Jesus, proportionate in their knowledge, identity, and action.

As I slip the little alien back into my Bible, I whisper to myself, "This Word is a Living Word, meant to be lived out in our day-to-day lives." This is not head knowledge; this is knowledge that comes by experience—knowing, being, and doing. Let's not grow aliens. Let's grow disciples.

Intentional Process

The most radical shift we can make in our understanding of discipleship is to move towards a life-long, intentional, process orientation. Rather than a quick fix or overnight metamorphosis, discipleship is a journey. We grow daily in relationship to God, in community with others, and in understanding our purpose. There will be ebbs and flows to each of these areas in our lives. There are times my soul feels so full of life, health, and strength that I can hardly contain the joy. There are other times my soul feels dry and my spiritual practice feels devoid of meaning. This is what it means to be a disciple. We yoke ourselves to Jesus and keep pressing forward. As Paul did, we remember to press on toward the goal for which Christ is calling us heavenward (Philippians 3:14). I live for this day and the next one. I am not defined by the past, nor do I live in the past. Yesterday's spirituality and vitality is not life for today.

I want to invite you, once again, to experience grace. To hear the Holy Spirit whisper, "Lay down your heavy burden of guilt and feelings of not-enoughness when it comes to your devotional life or relationship with Me. Many of us struggle with devotions. We struggle with discipleship. We struggle with prayer. We wish there was a "just do this," so the church will then be what it is called to be. There is no "silver bullet" or "this is the answer," though we wish there were.

There is *an* answer though. Trust in God's grace on the journey.

Walk with the One who loves us deeply and who won't let us go. This is not a cliché, but an expression of reality. The answer is not a program but a deeply personal God. The answer is not found in right religious practice, but in a growing relationship.

As people, and especially as leaders, it is tempting to look for "the fix," to seek that one thing that will solve the problem for ourselves and for those we serve. Instead of a fix, we are invited to turn again to fix our gaze on Jesus. We are invited on a journey.

Foundational Values

Discipleship is following Jesus. In the process of following, there are three key areas where growth occurs in the life of the disciple: (1) growth in our relationship with God, (2) nurturing relationships with others in community, and (3) developing purpose through witness and service on behalf of others. Three values, as you see here: God (first), Community, and Purpose. These three values serve as the foundation for the growth that happens during the 12-week discipleship course. Each exercise, interaction, and method is meant to facilitate growth in these key areas.

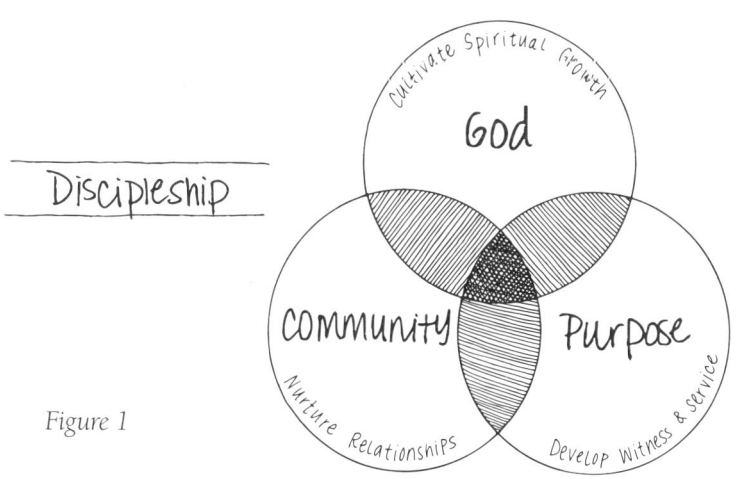

Figure 1

Come Out of Hiding

Jesus has broken the dividing wall between us and God, us and others, and even the divisions inside ourselves, leading to a greater understanding of our purpose. "For He Himself (Jesus) is our peace, who made both groups into one and broke down the barrier of the dividing wall" (Ephesians 2:14, NASB). God wants to bring us back to a place of oneness. Living this story of healing and wholeness in the world is a large part of what it means to be a disciple. This is evidenced in the discipleship journey in the invitation to the participants to be honest. There is no more separation, condemnation, or judgment because of the grace extended to us in Jesus. Because of this great gift, we can come out of hiding. Discipleship participants are invited to be honest with themselves, God, and others. This nurtures authenticity in sharing and is the fertile ground where growth and transformation can take place in relationship with God, community, and one's own purpose.

How We Grow

Experiential learning models highlight the facets of knowing, being, and doing as inseparable parts of a process that leads to growth. As the learner experiences information (*knowing*), reflects on it (*being*), and applies it to their life (*doing*), the result is a richer integration of change into the life of the learner.

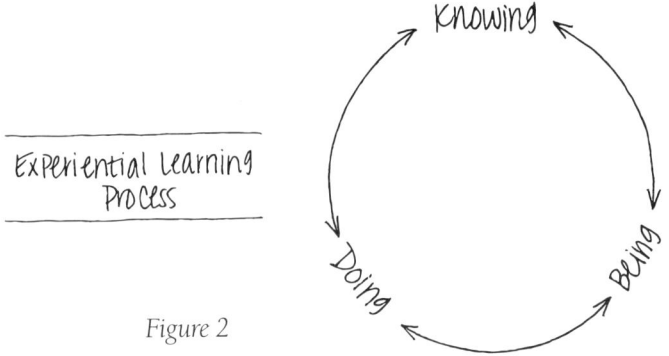

Figure 2

The relationship between the experiential learning process—knowing, being, doing—and discipleship is clear. Jesus' invitation to His disciples was, "Come, follow me" (Matthew 4:19) and "Learn from me" (Matthew 11:28-30). Jesus wanted His disciples to learn through an experience of shared life (Mark 3:14). In this process, they gained experiential knowledge about Jesus' ways (Mark 7:17; Acts 4:13), reflected in a change of heart and attitude (John 6:66-69, 13:1-9), and took action—doing and applying what Jesus taught them (Mark 6:7-13; Luke 10:1-12). The type of learning the disciples engaged in with Jesus was experiential.

Nonetheless, it is easy for humans to focus on knowledge alone. In one interchange with the teachers of the law, Jesus said, "You study the Scriptures diligently because you think that in them you possess eternal life. These are the very Scriptures that testify about me, yet you refuse to come to me to have life" (John 5:39-40). Knowledge of the Scriptures is intended to lead to a heart understanding of Jesus and the action of coming to Him which leads to life. Knowledge requires action (James 1:22). Jesus desires that disciples both hear and act on the word. "Therefore, everyone who hears these words of mine and puts them into practice is like a wise man who built his house on the rock" (Matthew 7:24).

Knowledge of doctrine, that is, biblical information about God, separated from a meaningful relationship with Jesus, produces self-sufficiency, self-righteousness, and self-centeredness (Matthew 23), characteristics seen in the New Testament descriptions of the Pharisees and the Scribes. However, in the context of an experiential relationship with Jesus, knowledge of doctrine becomes robust, leading to application in the context of real life. An experiential relationship with Jesus leads to the gospel in action (2 Peter 1:5-9). As believers learn to practice the ways of Jesus, they are kept from "being ineffective and unproductive in [their] knowledge of our Lord Jesus Christ" (2 Peter 1:8). Jesus desires that knowledge lead to the experience of producing effective, fruitful action in the life of the believer.

Gabe Lyons urges believers "to recover the Gospel, to relearn and fall in love again with that historic, beautiful, redemptive, faithful, demanding, reconciling, all-powerful, restorative, atoning, grace-abounding, soul-quenching, spiritually fulfilling good news of God's love."[1] This falling in love again with Jesus is at the heart of the experience of the disciple. Discipleship, as Jesus modeled it, allows the knowing, being, and doing aspects of Christian faith to find their rightful place in the life of the believer. Discipleship that embraces an experiential learning model recaptures what it means to follow Christ in the world today.

Discipleship is ultimately a work of the heart, the process of becoming more Christlike.[2] The primary role of the church, according to Jesus' Great Commission, is to make disciples of all people (Matthew 28:18-20). The church is to be a nucleus of disciple-making activity—instructing and mentoring believers and unbelievers alike in what it means to follow Jesus. This is best done experientially.

Discipleship is the answer to the questions of unbelievers and the inward need of believers. It offers the disciple purpose and resolves the disconnect between belief and practice. The call to discipleship is the clear invitation of Jesus to each Christian to incarnate the gospel in everyday life. This takes place as a result of being with Christ. Discipleship includes many facets of change in the life of the believer. It is this change the world desires to see. Over time, what takes place in the process of discipleship is a metamorphosis which transforms how individuals relate to themselves, God, others, and their purpose in the created world. This wholistic approach allows for a fuller transformation in the life of the believer.

Experiential Learning

The imperative for all three aspects of experiential learning in the discipleship process is found in the Great Commission. "To make disciples" means to make learners who follow after and experience the pattern of living Jesus set out. This is further clarified by the next part of the text: "to *teach* them to *do* all things I have commanded you" (emphasis added). The act of becoming a disciple of Jesus is, by its very nature, transformational and experiential. It is a complete shift in lifestyle. Experiential learning is what discipleship is all about. As Figure 2 outlines, one aspect of learning naturally leads to the other—knowing to being, being to doing, doing to knowing, and so on. As disciples experience knowing God and being transformed inwardly by the Holy Spirit, they will naturally do as God has commanded.

The goal of a discipleship process is to create space for learning on all three levels—knowing, being, and doing—in order to allow disciples to experience the power and change of God in their whole being. Rather than compartmentalizing growth, this allows disciples to be transformed by the Holy Spirit in every aspect of their lives through the disciple-making process. As the disciples are changed by Jesus, they are able to more faithfully and fruitfully represent Jesus in the world.

It is my sincere hope that we in the Seventh-day Adventist Church will recapture our focus on being and growing disciples. This emphasis on discipleship is the fulfillment of the Great Commission of Jesus. As we journey with members to embrace growth in their relationship with God, with others in community, and in living their purpose in this world, all three aspects of experiential learning are maximized. Knowledge is integrated into everyday life (knowing), reflection is evidence of greater emotional health and self-awareness (being), and both are lived out in the day-to-day experience and purpose of the disciple (doing). I have seen this growth through the experiential discipleship journey, *Deep Calling*.

Lift Up One Another

In Exodus 17:8-13, we find the Israelites were camped out at Rephidim. They had just left slavery. They were then in a dry and dusty place. They were tormented by thirst until the Lord instructed Moses to strike a rock and they were refreshed. Then, with only God's refreshment sustaining them, the Amalekites attacked.

Before we go any further in this story, something that is immediately clear is that if we are desperate, if we find ourselves dry and thirsty, God will provide for us. Many times, we are praying to leave the desperate place. We come alongside others and pray for God to lead them out of the dry place to safe, green pasture. Instead, in this instance, God offers gushing water *in* the dry place. The refreshment you seek could be exactly in the situation you're in, not by changing locations, but by finding streams in the desert.[3] It could be in the difficulty, in the marriage, in the friendship, or in the church you are struggling with.

Now, back to the battle. Joshua gathered men to fight, just as Moses told him to. Moses went to stand up on the hill. In his hand was the very staff that he had just used to strike the rock as God provided for the needs of the people to satisfy their thirst.

What the people experienced next was shocking. As long as Moses lifted his hands, they won. If he lowered his hands, they lost. Winning, losing, winning, losing. It didn't take long for them to recognize the pattern in what was happening in the battle.

We don't completely know the reason God chose to work this way in response to the raising of Moses' hands, but I can imagine God's delight in this posture of dependence and trust. Moses, with hands uplifted to the sky, was saying in the midst of an attack, "I don't know how this will all work out, but I am choosing to turn towards you in trust." Some of us need to remember this truth. We need to raise up our hands in prayer today and say, "I believe you are fighting for me, God." In our personal lives, our families, our organizations and churches, and in our small groups, we declare that God is at work!

It was working out quite well. With Moses' hands up, the battle was going fine. Then, he grew weary. He couldn't hold up his hands anymore. The enemy started to overpower Joshua and the men. Seeing this, his friends, Aaron and Hur, got him a rock to sit on and came to support Moses. Each one of them took one of his arms and held it up to the sky. Because of this strength and support, Moses' hands were held up the entire day. Joshua and the army defeated the army of Amalek.

The call of God is to live in community. We are not to be the lone person on the hill with our hands raised up, somehow with enough strength to hold steady, come what may. We aren't called to be the lone disciple-maker in our church, the one raising up a new perspective of discipleship in our church or church district. Instead, this story is a poignant visual of what it looks like to receive support. When I get tired, when I get discouraged, when I lose hope, that's when I need those around me. I have friends who stand with me in battle and who hold up my arms. We stay by each other through all of it.

There are times you feel like you're winning. There are other times you're weary and struggling. That's the power of doing life together. Together we come to raise hands and hearts in faith and in trust. Together we say, "You are God and I believe you are fighting for us." Together we seek God and press in towards our Maker.

God is the One who provides friends, leaders, and colleagues for us when we cannot hold up our arms anymore. I know you hold up other's arms. You are a leader—this is your calling. As a pastor, elder, chaplain, friend, spouse, or fellow believer, you come alongside and lift up arms. When overwhelming circumstances gnaw at the edges and anxiety threatens, you hold up others' arms.

The question I want to ask you is, "Who is holding up your arms?"

As you begin this journey of leading others in discipleship, who is holding up your arms? This discipleship journey is powerful, life-changing, and transformative, especially as you, the leader, experience what you are sharing with others. Who are you allowing to join you in your pain, weariness, and struggle?

The power of a community of faith is that we don't do it alone. There are times we pray and practice our faith and we feel everything; it's real to us—body, mind, and heart. Then there are other times you feel numb…broken…weary. It's then that others can hold up your hands and lift up your heart. When you can't hold up your hands, you need Aaron and Hur to come around you.

It's said that "we stand on the shoulders of the generations that went before us," and that's true. However, in this story, Moses' shoulders were held up by the people around him. It's not about the great leader on whose shoulders we are standing. Instead it's the story of how the arms of the "great person" were held up by the people on either side. This is what it means to live in community. It's not good that we do life or ministry alone. We are called to life together. We are called to be and grow disciples together.

May you see that God desires to grow you experientially in your relationship with God, community and purpose.

May you experience deep, caring community in your own life, even as you create this space for others.

May you be vulnerable enough to allow someone else to hold up your arms.

Discussion Questions

1. Which aspect of the experiential learning process—knowing, being, doing—do you need more of right now? What is one thing you can do today to share that experience with Jesus?
2. Where in your life, relationships, and church do you need God to provide water in dry places?
3. In what area of your life or ministry are you trying to be the lone person on the hill with your hands raised up? Who is someone like Aaron or Hur whom you can invite to hold up your arms in support?

CHAPTER NINE

Eight Calls to a Deeper Life

"You can't think your way into new habits. New habits can only emerge as you practice them. This is the most challenging part. Practice is the small ordinary path to transformation."

JAMES K. A. SMITH

WHEN OUR SON WAS 3 ½ YEARS OLD, he commented on our citrus trees as we were leaving the house. "Mom, look at those two old pomelos that fell down from the tree." I acknowledged what he saw and he quickly asked a question, as kids do so well.

"Why does the fruit fall from the tree? It's too yucky and old to eat. Why does it fall down?"

I explained to him that the tree has to let go of the old fruit in order to have room for new fruit to grow. As I said these words, I realized the implications for my life, and for the life of the church.

God's voice whispered in my heart, "That's what I want to do in you. You just let go of the old because I want to grow the new fruit of the Spirit in your life."

Maybe there are things in your life that you want to change. Maybe there are things in the life of your church that weigh heavily on your shoulders and on your heart. Maybe you find yourself with a deep hunger for the new fruit of the Spirit in your life, your church, or your organization. Whatever your experience is now, wherever your church or organization is now, God can grow new fruit in your life and in the life of your church or organization. You and I have to acknowledge the old and let it go. Surrender it, letting it drop to the ground. God is growing new fruit. Like the tree planted by the water that bears fruit in season (Psalm 1), God wants you to have an ever-renewed experience with God, and lead others into the same experience.

How does God develop that experience in us? In my life and ministry, I have seen God work through eight calls—habits we grow in our lives which help us respond to God. These are the eight calls that the discipleship curriculum, *Deep Calling*, is built on.

- **A Call to Devotion:** living in a daily rhythm of love.
- **A Call to Prayer:** engaging in conversations with God as a friend.
- **A Call to Rest:** experiencing Sabbath restoration.
- **A Call to Community:** entering into life together.
- **A Call to Healing:** finding wholeness in the midst of our brokenness.
- **A Call to Witness:** discovering our call to own and tell our story.
- **A Call to Serve:** joining Jesus in incarnational ministry and mission.
- **A Call to Bless:** celebrating life with a prophetic voice, speaking what is not, as though it were.

These are the loving invitations of God that meet our deepest hunger and desire. "The heart of God yearns over His earthly children with a love stronger than death," Ellen White implores.[1] This love of God is what draws us, works within us, and ultimately changes our lives.

Longing for an Experience

James Rutz and the Gallup organization have found that "a significant number of 'unchurched' Americans feel there is not enough emphasis on spiritual experiences in the churches...churches have lost the spiritual part of religion."[2] There is a hunger for the practice of spirituality. Religion as a practice of the mind has dominated the practice of the heart, leaving people with a longing for connection with God.[3] I have seen this firsthand in pastoral ministry over the years. People desire an experience, the real-life practice of spirituality. I have seen in many Adventist church members an inability to move from faith as an informational understanding of a set of beliefs, to a relational practice that integrates truth into daily living. This has left them feeling unfulfilled and is, arguably, the most significant contributor to their restless search for answers and longing for greater depth of spiritual experience.

People have grown exhausted with just *doing church* or *going through the motions*. Religious experience has left church members empty, dry, and hungry for more. A. Allan Martin identifies the resulting dissatisfaction as "sacred discontent."[4] He points out that this discontent or hunger for more can be useful, even devotional, if it pushes us past superficial religion towards more of God.

Spiritual Habits

The first practical question that must be addressed is *what makes the difference between someone who is a Christian and someone who is not?* The number one distinction of Christians is that they are individuals who are *with* Christ. Disciples (or apprentices) are those who are with Jesus and who are seeking to become like Him. They live their lives asking this question: If Jesus were living my life, what would He do?[5] A relationship with Jesus must be maintained as the most important part of the disciple's life. Dietrich Bonhoeffer, the great Christian pastor and martyr in Germany during Nazi rule, distills this truth by saying, "The heart of the disciple must be set upon Christ alone."[6]

But how? How do we set our heart on Jesus? The most ancient of all recognized ways of transformation takes place through the practice of spiritual devotional habits or disciplines. As we hear the eight calls of God in our lives, we respond by developing habits that nurture space for response to God. **These habits that we can practice in our lives make room for the grace of God. We don't make the rainstorm,[7] just as we don't manufacture God's grace. Instead, we do something that puts us in the place where we can get wet by the rainstorm.** That's a spiritual habit: heeding the call of God to practice our faith with action.

The spiritual disciplines are the ways that God works in people's lives to transform them into who they are meant to be. By spending time in God's Presence, a person becomes someone with a worldview in line with the Kingdom of God.[8] The number and names of the spiritual disciplines vary depending on the source, but their purpose remains the same. The goal is to engage believers in a transformational process that allows them to become more like Christ. They are intentional methods used to focus the believers' attention on Jesus. There are seven practices that are included in most lists: Prayer, Meditation, Study, Fasting, Solitude/Silence, Worship, and Service.[9] These spiritual disciplines are often called the "classical disciplines" because they are central and foundational to the Christian life.[10]

Dallas Willard breaks down the classical disciplines into two categories: disciplines of abstinence (solitude, silence, fasting, etc.) and disciplines of engagement (study, worship, service, prayer, etc.). Seeing the disciplines within these two categories helps the believer to address sins of commission (things they are doing) and omission (things they are not doing)[11] Lauren Winner offers contemporary reflections from a Christian perspective on Jewish spiritual practices and disciplines. Her work emphasizes the prevalent desire to develop rhythms and meaning in spiritual practice. Spiritual disciplines fill the need for structure and deepened connection.[12]

In a sermon given in Switzerland in 1885, Ellen White expressed that:

> Faith and works go hand in hand; they act harmoniously in the work of overcoming. Works without faith are dead, and faith without works is dead. Works will never save us; it is the merit of Christ that will avail in our behalf. Through faith in Him, Christ will make all our imperfect efforts acceptable to God. The faith we are required to have is not a do-nothing faith; saving faith is that which works by love and purifies the soul.[13]

As disciples put into practice what they can do to connect with Christ and what they can avoid to make space for more of Christ in their life, transformation takes place by the work of the Holy Spirit. The goal is to develop habits and routines that bring ourselves, and other believers, into closer contact with Christ.

The purpose of devotional practices is for believers to experience God and be formed as disciples, alone and in community. These practices of connecting with God meet our deepest longing for spiritual experience and are the means by which we experience transformation.

The Miracle

It's important for us to remember that the power to produce an experience or change in our lives does not come from ourselves. S. Joseph Kidder draws needed attention to the role of the Holy Spirit. He writes, "The shift in the disciples did not result from some seminar they took in leadership or evangelism, or from some sort of self-improvement course, but as a result of the presence of the transformational power of the Holy Spirit."[14]

As birth is a miracle, so the discipleship process is a miracle. It is the mystery of God transforming disciples through the Holy Spirit's power.[15] Disciples are not able to control the process any more than babies are able to control their own birth. They do, however, see the effects of the miracle of transformation. The role of believers is to bring themselves to Jesus with the full knowledge that they cannot change themselves.[16] I believe it is in acknowledging this very truth—we as disciples are unable to change ourselves—that we experience our greatest transformation. Giving up control is often the hardest spiritual practice for the disciple.[17]

Ellen White says, "While the work of the Spirit is silent and imperceptible, its effects are manifest. If the heart has been renewed by the Spirit of God, the life will bear witness to the fact."[18] The silent and quiet work of the Spirit is happening in your life and mine as we surrender. "So, we have nothing in ourselves of which to boast. We have no ground for self-exaltation. Our only ground of hope is in the righteousness of Christ imputed to us, and in that wrought by His Spirit working in and through us."[19] Transformation is the work of God alone, done in the process of discipleship throughout the believer's life.

The experience of discipleship must be recaptured as our primary focus—as individuals and as a church. Bill Hull emphasizes this by saying, "Discipleship isn't just *one* of the things the church does; it *is* what the church does."[20]

We are called to live in a devotional rhythm. We are called to prayer as a conversation with God as a friend. We are called to experience the depth of Sabbath rest. We are called to live in community. We are called to healing, miraculously finding repair in the midst of our brokenness. We are called to witness to the power of God by telling our story. We are called to serve others incarnationally, just as Jesus did. We are called to bless—celebrating and calling out life that does not yet exist. These are the eight calls of God on our lives.

I invite you on a journey as we explore these calls and the transforming work of the Holy Spirit through habits we practice in response to the grace of God. It may require a reorientation of our priorities and our focus, individually and collectively as a church community. However, I believe it will be worth it as we witness new fruit of the Spirit in our own lives and the lives of those around us.

Back to What Matters Most

We traveled this past summer, preaching, and then spending time together as a family. We explored beaches and hiked in forests in British Columbia, Washington, Oregon, and California. There was beauty all around us. Bright spots of joy everywhere. Our Maker's handiwork on full display.

Only a few days into our trip, our 16-month-old daughter Ava took a leap in her language development. She pointed at things around her and said their names with recognition and assurance. Beyond the words she was already using like "Daddy" "Mommy" and "Siah" (her brother), she called out "Jesus," "baby," "book," "water," "hungry," "eat." Everything had a name and she would attempt to say it! She woke up.

One of the moments I hope always to remember is when I coached her at bedtime.

Say, "Jesus," I said.

"Jesus," she said.

Say, "loves," I said.

"Loves," she said.

Then before I could say the next word, she called out with such joy, her eyes dancing:

"Me!"

It caught me by surprise. She was delighted in her ability to fill in the sentence with the next word! More than that, she seemed delighted by what she was announcing.

"Jesus loves me!" she said slowly, in a sweet baby voice.

Yes, my darling! It's true.

We repeated this pattern a few times. Each time, she filled in with great joy, "me!" before I was able to say it.

In the stillness of that room, a temporary home away from home, I blessed my daughter. With tears brimming in my eyes for the sheer delight and gift of the moment:

My daughter, may you always know you are deeply loved by Jesus.

May you remember that you bring this same delight to us and to God.

May you know that your presence brings joy and makes the world a better place.

What about you dear friend? Do you need to go back to the basics today? Remember the invitation of God, and God's desire to live life with you. Rediscover what matters most. Delight in the sheer simplicity of the truth: You are deeply loved by Jesus. God delights in you. Your presence brings joy and makes the world a better place.

The invitation of God, these eight calls to a deeper life, all begin here. With the reality of how God feels about each one of us. Discipleship is, after all, a response to the grace of God at work in our lives.

Knowing we are loved and delighted in is the beginning of the new fruit God longs to grow in your life, and in your church. Everything begins with realizing how loved you are. Won't you respond to this call of Love?

May you know you are deeply loved by Jesus. You bring delight to God.

May you know that your presence makes the world a better place.

May you create life-giving spaces where others can respond to the love and call of God in their own lives.

Discussion Questions

1. What old fruit is God calling you to let go of in order for the new fruit of the Spirit to grow in your life?
2. Which one or two of the eight calls of God has contributed most to your spiritual growth? Which one do you want to experience more of?
3. What is one way you've experienced the love of Jesus recently? What is one way your presence makes the world a better place?

CHAPTER TEN

A Call to Devotion: Daily Rhythm of Love

"Attention is the beginning of devotion."

MARY OLIVER

MANY YEARS AGO, I RECEIVED AN EMAIL advertisement inviting me to turn my old shirts into a quilt. Sending in my shirts would give me the gift of a gorgeous memory quilt and would, at the same time, provide work for a United States war veteran. I sorted and chose a couple dozen shirts for inclusion in the quilt. One of those shirts flooded my mind with memories of the time my husband Caleb and I spent in a long-distance relationship.

We met at Southwestern Adventist University while on a leadership retreat with the chaplain's office. Caleb was the drama director and I was the student chaplain that year. We were immediately drawn to one another and wanted to talk. Fortunately for us, we were paired off by the head chaplain to be partners throughout the retreat. After a whirlwind school year and beautiful months of dating, I graduated and left to begin ministry in Washington state. Caleb continued in Texas for his last year of undergraduate studies. We didn't have cell phones so there was no texting or Facetime or calls at any time of the day. There was no social media where we kept up with each other's day. But we did talk on the phone using calling cards and we wrote letters—yes, real letters with paper and pen.

Throughout these months apart, I was forming a plan to see Caleb and surprise him. I bought a ticket to Texas. Not only that, I talked to the men's dean and asked if I could have a group of our friends join me in Caleb's dorm room so that at the end of the day, he could be completely shocked. The dean agreed. We all snuck up the hallway and hid in his room. Balloons filled the room so when Caleb entered, he thought our friends were surprising him. He smiled and thanked them. Then, I stepped out from behind the door. Surprise!!

The long distance afforded us time to write, talk, and grow in our relationship. It was good. Our love grew and deepened. But there was nothing like that hug, looking into each other's eyes, and seeing each other face-to-face. It was a great weekend—one I will always remember. Before leaving for this trip, I bought a special outfit to wear for the surprise—the shirt of that outfit is now sewn into the memory quilt. This square in my quilt reminds me of what it's like to love from a distance and to experience sweet reunion.

We live in a long-distance relationship with God here on earth. As we live in love with God, we practice a life of devotion by the power of the Holy Spirit. Hope within us loves the One we can't see, even as we wait for the day when we will see face-to-face. We have hope in the present and a hope for what is to come.

The first call of God is to live a life of devotion. A life of devotion recognizes that the life of the follower of Jesus is more the gift of what God has given to you and less what you are doing for God. We must make space for the work of God in our lives; however, we do not do the work ourselves. **Devotion is a rhythm of life that is characterized by love.** The ways that we practice relating to God in love shape our hearts, character, and actions. How do we form a life of devotion as we live in a relationship with God? Consider developing a rule of life, prioritizing time in God's Word, and approaching it all with joy.

Rule of Life

The *Rule of Life* brings together the practice of the spiritual disciplines, the understanding of emotional health, and the knowledge of self into a spiritual rhythm that encourages the process of change. Barton describes:

> A rule of life is a way of ordering our life around the values, practices and relationships that keep us open and available to God for the work of spiritual transformation that only God can bring about. Simply put, a rule of life provides structure and space for our growing.[1]

Scazzero summarizes the *Rule of Life* as "an intentional, conscious plan to keep God at the center of everything we do. . . . The starting point and foundation of any Rule is a desire to be with God."[2] The concept of the *Rule of Life* is a valuable way of reordering one's life to follow the ways and priorities of Jesus, instead of one's own, or those given by others. This becomes even more important in the increasingly fast-paced world of today. The focus must be on structuring life around God's priorities instead of my own, making central a relationship with Jesus amidst the distractions of secular and religious life.

In chapter 8 of the book *Steps to Christ*, entitled "Growing Up into Christ," Ellen White shares her understanding of what it looks like to grow in Christ. She marks the difference between justification and sanctification in the life of the Christian. While justification takes place the moment we receive the gift of God's grace, sanctification takes a lifetime. "The plants and flowers grow not by their own care or anxiety or effort, but by receiving that which God has furnished to minister to their life. The child cannot, by any anxiety or power of its own, add to its stature. No more can you, by anxiety or effort of yourself, secure spiritual growth."[3]

Growth in our lives comes as we "abide in Christ." What does this abiding in Christ look like in your life? White goes on to say, "You are just as dependent upon Christ, in order to live a holy life, as is the branch upon the parent stock for growth and fruitfulness. Apart from Him you have no life."[4] Everything that is lasting comes from remaining connected to Jesus.

The *rule of life* is a way of intentionally abiding in Christ. What does this look like practically? Here are three examples from my *rule of life*. One of the guidelines in my *rule of life* about abiding in Jesus is that I do not check email or social media before time in devotion with God in the morning. It's too easy for me to get caught up in focusing on what I have to do that day, or in other relationships, and my intention is to fix my eyes on Jesus (Hebrews 12). Does this mean I do this perfectly every day? No. There are times I miss this and absentmindedly grab my phone after being awakened earlier than I intended (can you tell our kids are young?). Yet, over the course of time, this habit is forming my way of abiding in Christ.

I have made a commitment to be formed and shaped by time in the Word of God each day. This time in the Scriptures has changed my life. What do I read? For the last 15 years, I have read one psalm each day, in addition to reading from the Gospels. These prayers of praise and lament have expressed the words of my heart in different seasons of my life. They have shaped me in profound ways.

Another part of my *rule of life* is a commitment to retreat and to relationship. Each year I take a day in the spring and a day in the fall in silent prayer with God, unplugged from social media and email. In addition, I take one spiritual retreat in community with friends where we intentionally spend time in prayer, the Word, and open up to one another about the work of God in our lives. We've been practicing this commitment to retreat for nine years now. This has shaped the way that I abide in Christ and has been transformational in my life.

We all have ways that we live. Whether thought through intentionally or unintentionally, we develop patterns of living. As you reflect on and create your rule of life, look for ways and rhythms that help you to abide in Christ. Commit to these patterns of devotion.

Even as we develop a rule of life, we must remember that there is no part of this that we do on our own. Ellen White admonishes, "Many have an idea that they must do some part of the work alone. They have trusted in Christ for the forgiveness of sin, but now they seek by their own efforts to live aright. But every such effort must fail."[5] It is God's call, love, presence, and invitation to partner in mission that shape what it means to be a follower of Jesus. It is God's work from beginning to end. **Even as we make space for the work God is doing, it will always be the work of God.**

The Word of God

Time in the Scriptures has been a daily part of my devotion to Jesus and has provided an avenue of transformation. Scripture was inspired by God—"God-breathed" (2 Timothy 3:16-17). The Spirit who hovered over creation as it was dark, formless, and void (Genesis 1) is the same Spirit who hovered over ordinary people who were moved to write the Holy Scriptures. Even now, that same Spirit hovers over you and me to create something new in us (Romans 12:2). True worship is about giving our whole lives in response to the mercy of God. The logical response, Paul says, is to let our lives be structured and shaped daily by grace. To come to the Word and be changed.

One of the greatest dangers is to separate – bifurcate – our spiritual life from the rest of our lives – the spiritual world from the material world. God wants to renew our minds. The same mind that pays the bills, reads the Scriptures, worships God, and watches TV. God wants us to bring our whole selves to experience the renewing of our minds.

This is a beautiful part of the Adventist message. There is a whole-life focus to our message. All of you is loved. All of you is invited into a relationship. All of you is renewed. Through the power of the Scriptures and the regenerating work of the Spirit, you are in the process of transformation. It doesn't happen automatically. There is no finish line to this. God's Spirit comes to abide and reside in you and that brings a new way of thinking and orienting your life. Day by day, for the rest of your life.

The people of God who were used for the sacred work of writing the Scriptures wrote in their own language, time, and place. They wrote as the Spirit moved them with thoughts. What we hold now in the Bible is incredible work. It has contexts and times, and yet it is timeless. It reflects what the people understood then, and yet it applies to us now. God has always been about incarnation. The Holy Spirit incarnate in these ordinary, yet sacred, words. Jesus incarnate in the body of a man. Divine and yet human. The Holy Spirit incarnate now in us, the people of God.

This is why we hold onto hope. We firmly believe this radical truth that change is possible. Transformation, becoming something different than we are today, is possible. The Spirit is here. The way you are today is not the way you must be tomorrow. The way the church is now is not the way the church will always be. The hurting, suffering, and pain that exists now is not the way it will always be. This is true of the future promise of God in the coming of Jesus, but also true of the way the people of God are able to relieve the suffering of those around us today.

God invites us to bring our whole selves. Each day, I come to open myself up to God. I come to the Bible and I ask God to speak and move, form and shape my life through this Word by the same Spirit that inspired it. I am humble. Allowing Someone outside of me to master me. Scripture is not something to master, but something to be mastered by.[6] The grand theme of Scripture is relating the story of redemption; God's revelation to humanity and great rescue plan have been unfolding over thousands of years. I am a part of this story. We are a part of this story. When I read Scripture and let these words, stories, and experiences between God and God's people touch me, I get to respond as a part of this unbroken history of the people of God. I am taught and shaped, informed and transformed by this story, and by the Holy God who meets me here.

As I approach this word, I return to three questions that have shaped my reading of Scripture and my life. **What does this say? How does it connect with my life? Is there an invitation?**[7] So many times, I find, like Jacob, that "God was in this place and I didn't even realize it" (Genesis 28:16-19). It is this discovery of God that has brought my heart great joy.

Joy of Devotion

Harvey Cox says, that the modern person has been pressed "so hard toward useful work and rational calculation he has all but forgotten the joy of ecstatic celebration."[8] Even believers in Christ can easily forget that "the joy of the Lord is our strength" (Nehemiah 8:10).

Celebration is at the heart of the way of Christ. Jesus entered the world with a high note of jubilation (Luke 2:10). Jesus' first miracle was at a wedding feast (John 2). Jesus spoke joy to the disciples, even saying that he would make their joy complete (John 15:11). Jesus inaugurated His ministry, proclaiming the year of Jubilee

(Luke 4:18-19), canceling all debts, releasing all slaves, planting no crops (giving the land a rest), and returning property to the original owner. These all celebrated the provision of God!

We fight through physical barriers with sports or physical training, with piano lessons or with learning any new skill, all because we experience joy as a result. People struggle through school to reach their degree or certificate which qualifies them to do what they are called to do. Couples adjust to the first difficult years, looking forward to the gift of the rest of life together. If you don't experience joy, you won't keep something going for long.

Without joy and celebration, the spiritual disciplines become lifeless. Joy comes in obedience to Christ, even as discipline and habits are sometimes difficult to develop. Though it is a journey with highs and lows, joy comes through living our best possible life in Christ.

Ellen White says it this way in her classic book on Christian growth, *Steps to Christ*:

> Have there not been some bright spots in your experience? Have you not had some precious seasons when your heart throbbed with joy in response to the Spirit of God? When you look back into the chapters of your life experience do you not find some pleasant pages? Are not God's promises, like the fragrant flowers, growing beside your path on every hand? Will you not let their beauty and sweetness fill your heart with joy?[9]

Our minds and hearts need this focus on joy.

The life of the Christian is a life of joy. The life of Jesus' disciples is one of celebration. Even though we live in a world full of darkness, of suffering in which we often participate, we live with the confidence that God has overcome the darkness. Jesus told his disciples, "In this world you will have troubles, but rejoice, I have overcome the world" (John 16:33). Nouwen writes that we celebrate because "we see that God, not the Evil One, has the last word."[10]

God's people are those, as Eugene Peterson writes, "whose lives are bordered on one side by a memory of God's acts and the other by hope in God's promises, and who along with whatever else is happening, are able to say, at the center, 'We are one happy people.'"[11]

Our call to devotion is one of obedience and joy. If you aren't experiencing joy in Jesus, ask God for this gift of joy. It's a daily rhythm that we are invited into.

Hope Fulfilled

Our relationship with God is long-distance right now. Though the Spirit is with us and we speak to God daily, we don't see God face-to-face as we will in the day that is coming. It's just not the same as it will be then. "I go to prepare a place for you," Jesus said. I'm making a space for you. There will come a day when we will be fully together (John 14:1-3).

The day is coming when there will be a reunion of epic proportions. When our lives of devotion, love, and trust will see the One whom our hearts desire. Fullness of restoration, healing, and rejoicing is coming. When all things are made right once more. We were made for this. I simply cannot wait. Until then, may our lives be characterized by devotion and transformation, even as we actively live out our hope.

May you rest deeply in the work of Christ in your life.

May you develop a rule of life that guides your living in devotion to God with intentionality.

May you find joy in living a life of devotion, inspiring others to do the same.

Discussion Questions

1. What is one practice you'd like to add to your rule of life?
2. In what ways have the Scriptures called you into a whole-life focus?
3. What is one area of your life in which you'd like more joy? Take a moment to ask God for this gift in Jesus.

CHAPTER ELEVEN

A Call to Prayer: Conversation with God

"To be a Christian without prayer is no more possible than to be alive without breathing."

MARTIN LUTHER

DO YOU EVER FEEL LIKE YOUR PRAYERS aren't getting above the ceiling and that your prayer life is boring and dead? Maybe it's because your lifestyle is so completely contained that you really don't need God. When you hit a crisis point, you suddenly feel a passion and drive towards prayer, but then other times, you're not even interested. When we realize that in order to live a life that honors God, we need God moment by moment, our prayer life begins to change. When we realize that God desires a loving, open relationship with us, prayer grows to be as natural for us as breathing.

One of our friends was so excited to finally get a new cell phone: the latest iPhone from Apple. He called to ask me some questions about how to use his phone, since he had never owned that kind of phone before. I shared with him a few things and before I could finish my tutorial, he got really excited. He exclaimed, "I didn't even know what I had!" I didn't even know what I had. Isn't that true with us? We don't even realize the gift we have in prayer.

What is Prayer?

In the devotional book *Steps to Christ*, Ellen White says, "Prayer is the opening of the heart to God as to a friend."[1] The gift of prayer is the avenue of connection we have with the Living God. Prayer is looking to the Lord and seeking God's face and strength (1 Chronicles 16:11). Prayer is about the intention and choice to connect, both talking with and listening to God.

Prayer is the second most referenced spiritual practice in the Bible. The first is praise. The Scriptures are filled with examples of prayer, dialogue about prayer, and imperatives to pray. As Spurgeon points out, we open the Bible and read, "All began to call on the name of the Lord;"[2] and just as we are about to close the book, we read the "Amen" of the closing prayer. Prayer in the Scriptures is seen from beginning to end.

Throughout the ages, Christ followers have relied on prayer as a way to connect with God and grow deeper in relationship with God. As M. Robert Mulholland Jr. said, "Prayer is the act by which the people of God become incorporated into the presence and action of God in the world."[3] In prayer, I understand more deeply who God is, who I am, and what I am called to be or to do this day that I have been given to live in this world.

As we read and hear prayer stories from others, we may begin to ask questions about our prayer life as leaders and wonder what prayer can look like in our lives today. On day one, we say we will pray for one hour, and after 10 minutes, we're done. Or you find yourself with the weight of ministry and life on your shoulders and you grow distracted from what you know you need: time with Jesus. When we fall short, we tend to beat ourselves up and just give up.

I believe it can help us immensely when we shift from prayer as something to do, to prayer as a conversation with our Creator. God desires a relationship with you, and prayer is the avenue for communication, ongoing throughout our day and our lives. When we come to God in prayer before running to the demands of life or even in the midst of days full of responsibility, our identity becomes rooted in Love (Ephesians 3:17).

Prayer in the Life of Jesus

How do we respond to those things in our lives which are unplanned and unanticipated?

Throughout the gospels we see that this constantly happened in the life of Christ. A woman came up to Him on His way to raise a dead little girl to life and He stopped and healed her. Two blind men called out, interrupting His journey, and Jesus stopped to heal them. People brought their babies to be blessed by Him, interrupting what He was doing, and He stopped everything to bless them. This happened again and again to Jesus. What kept Jesus grounded, able to answer definitively "yes" or "no" to these opportunities that came His way? One word: prayer.

Mark 1:35 says, "Very early in the morning, while it was still dark, Jesus got up, left the house and went off to a solitary place, where he prayed."

Jesus prayed and sought direction from the Lord. He was guided in those quiet moments and able to discern where God would have Him go. In the next verses, when the disciples came to rush Him off into the activity of those who were seeking Him, His answer was, no, it's time for us to move on to the nearby villages. How did Jesus know that this interruption was not for Him? From the time He had spent with God.

When we experience God in prayer, we open ourselves up to be guided through the expected and unexpected of our day. In prayer we hear where and when and how to go about living now, giving us perspective to take each moment as what it is: truly a gift from God.

Henri Nouwen had a life-altering interaction with one of his professors. It was from this conversation that he went on to write:

> It has been the interruptions to my everyday life that have most revealed to me the divine mystery of which I am a part. All of these interruptions presented themselves as opportunities; invited me to look in a new way at my identity before God. Each interruption took something away from me; each interruption offered something new.[4]

Isn't it like this for us sometimes? The thing which you don't want to do, that which seems to be distracting you, ends up being a step towards your goal, the fulfillment of a dream, or the realization of another piece of God's purpose coming together in your life. Prayer opens the door of connection with God, giving guidance for all that fills our days.

Prayer in Scripture

The Bible contains 650 definite prayers, expressed in many different ways.[5] In fact, the first thing we observe about prayer in the Bible is the tremendous diversity. We see collective prayers at the temple dedication, while in the midst of crisis, or at gatherings. The book of Acts mentions prayer or praying over 30 times. God moves and works among the people, and the church seems to be growing by prayer.

We see personal prayers. We experience joy and pain as the people of God call out to God. We find Jacob wrestling with God (Genesis 32:22-32). We see Esther requesting everyone to fast (and pray) as she took action on behalf of her people (Esther 4). We hear the heartfelt prayers of David recorded in the Psalms. We experience

Hannah's honesty and anguish as she poured out her heart in prayer (1 Samuel 1:10-16). In the New Testament, Mary's prayer of praise fills our hearts with joy (Luke 1:47-50); we celebrate the miracle when God freed Peter from jail in response to the prayers of the people of God (Acts 12); and we lament with Paul who pleaded with God in prayer, but instead of receiving what he asked for, is given grace and strength (2 Corinthians 12).

As we notice the variety in the prayers recorded in Scripture, we can't help but also experience the honesty of these prayers. The openness and vulnerability that characterize the relationships the people shared with their God is grounding. "My God, why have you forsaken me?" is a prayer found in the Psalms and heard later from the mouth of Jesus as He was suffering on the cross.

As Dr. Allan Walshe said during our class discussion one day, "God would rather have us complain honestly instead of praise falsely." God already knows everything. Being honest in God's presence can't hurt us; it can only help open us to God's healing and love. The invitation from God is to find new ways to pray and connect with God. Pray as much as you can honestly, authentically pray. In these stories of prayer, in the diversity and in the raw honesty, we are compelled towards the sacred call and necessity of prayer.

Ways to Pray

Taking the two observations, variety and honesty, what does it look like to engage with God in prayer in some of the ways recorded in the Bible? Here are several that you can try in your own life of devotion and with your church or organization.

Pray the Scriptures
There are treasured passages of Scripture that I come back to, not only to say, but also to pray. The 23rd Psalm is one of those. I can go through each verse, imagining the Good Shepherd and how God is

speaking into my life through these words. Psalm 91 is another such passage, where I call out to God as my refuge and my rest. There have been seasons of my life where I have prayed the Lord's Prayer every day as a way of connecting with the heart of God and God's intentions for humanity. Finding Scriptures to pray daily can enrich our spiritual lives and broaden our vocabulary in prayer.

Lift Up Your Hands
Have you ever seen someone with their hands raised up in prayer or in worship? What's that all about? This was a common Semitic posture of prayer. Lamentations 3:41 declares, "We lift up our heart and hands toward God in heaven." In the Psalms, there are numerous references to lifting up hands in prayer before God (Psalms 28:2; 63:4; 141:1, 2). Paul instructed Timothy that he desired the "lifting up of holy hands in prayer" (1 Timothy 2:8). What is it about raising up our hands that would aid in our connection to God in prayer or in praise?

I will never forget how my two-year-old daughter, Ava, runs over to me when I get home and stretches out both her hands, raising them up to greet me. It completely melts my heart. It's the sweetest thing to have a child raise their hands to you, isn't it? What is the child desiring? If you're an uncle or aunt, mom or dad, grandpa or grandma, you might know this means, "Pick me up!" or "I want to be held by you!" Our Ava says, "Hold you?" when she wants to be held, arms stretched up reaching for me.

I think God loves to see our arms outstretched in prayer and in praise. James 4:8 says, "Draw near to God and God will draw near to you!" This is one of the first verses that I memorized when I became a Christian, the promise that God will always draw near.

There are days I stretch up my hands in prayer and say, "God I'm raising my hands up to you, like Ava raises up her hands to be picked up. I need you." I pray in the midst of difficulty with hands raised up. I don't understand what is happening in my life or the lives of those I love. Some days I lift up my hands because my heart is so full of praise because of a victory God has worked. I raise up my hands to celebrate! I hold up my hands, cheering for the goodness of God I have just witnessed! Raising up my hands has opened up new experiences in my prayer and praise of God.

Prayer Cards for Intercession

There is a wonderful suggestion from the book *A Praying Life* by Paul Miller in regards to how to engage in intercessory prayer in a practical way.[6] I've been blessed as I have used prayer cards over the years. You take index cards and on each one, put the name of a person you want to pray for at the top. Ask God to lead you to a passage for them. Write out the verse and specific prayers for them below. Leave space for when these prayers are answered, along with the date when you saw God working in this area of their lives. You can take these prayer cards with you wherever you go. On my phone, I have prayer lists for intercession in *Slack* and *Evernote*,[7] which allow me to pray for others in the in-between moments. In my office I have a prayer bulletin board where I have pictures of people I pray for daily, as well as notecards with different requests. It can be affirming to see God work in the lives of people you're praying for and in your prayer time. When I look at the stack of cards where I've written "answered" and the date God worked, it reaffirms God's presence in my life.

All Your Senses

The first Epistle of John launches with the most earnest of declarations. The energy in the text is palpable. First John 1:1-4 proclaims that we have seen something with our own eyes… with our own hands we have touched it… we have heard it ourselves and it has made all the difference… Eternal life has been revealed. The subject of the passage rips through the text, a ballistic path from the very beginning, through the present and into the future, breaking down any barriers between the tenses. This has made all the difference for the disciples! They have experienced it with all of their senses and the connection has changed them. As we make time to behold God, we are invited into an experience that makes full use of all our senses (seeing, hearing, touching, tasting, smelling).

What can you do this week to put yourself in a place where you can experience God? Hearing, seeing, and touching the Word of Life? Is there a song you can pray? Is there a prayer you can paint, collage, or draw? Is there prayer time that is experienced with candles lit and the smell of incense or oils, reminiscent of the Old Testament sanctuary (Exodus 30:34-38; 37:2). Are there ways you can experience the holiness of God, capturing each scene of the Scriptures with not just your mind, but all your senses?

John invited the gathered crowd to "Behold, the Lamb of God who takes away the sin of the world!" (John 1:29). The author of Hebrews declared, "Let us fix our eyes on Jesus, the author and finisher of our faith" (Hebrews 12:1-2). As we behold and fix our eyes, we are invited to do so with the full range of our sensory experience. This will enliven our prayer life.

Gratitude and Praise

In Philippians 4:11-13, Paul counseled us not to wait until everything is settled in our lives to experience happiness. Don't postpone joy and gladness until your situation changes or until you have acquired a certain thing. If you cannot be happy now, you will not be happy then. Happiness is not a matter of what you have, or what situation you are in; it's a matter of who you are and how you respond to life. Gratitude generates joy.

To live in gratitude is to acknowledge that, at the core, we are satisfied by God's Presence alone. As the psalmist said, "I will see your face; when I awake, I will be satisfied with seeing your likeness" (Psalm 17:15). For the followers of Jesus, Thanksgiving is not just a holiday or a season, but a way of life. The same root word for communion (eucharist) is to give thanks. We come to the table to receive the sacrificial death of Jesus and live in His life. This "giving thanks" becomes the way that I live.

Expressing gratitude and praise has changed my prayer life. Almost every day, I take time to thank God for the gifts I see in my life. Often, it's not until I stop to show gratitude that I realize there are gifts I would have missed altogether if it weren't for this regular practice. In addition, I take time to praise God for who God is—the characteristics and qualities of God that I experience: God's love, faithfulness, trustworthiness, and grace. Taking time to see God for who God is lifts my heart up in praise! Psalm 89:15 implores, "Blessed are those who have learned to acclaim you, who walk in the light of your presence, O Lord." As I learn this habit of acclaiming and finding joy in God during prayer, I am not the same person I was.

Be Still

Most of our prayer is talking to and/or intercessory prayer with God. However, listening is also a key part of prayer. Words are not always necessary for our hearts to pray. "Be still," the psalmist entreats, "Know that I am God" (Psalm 46:10).

In *Ministry of Healing*, Ellen White beautifully describes where we can find this stillness with God.

> All who are under the training of God need the quiet hour for communion with their own hearts, with nature, and with God… We must individually hear Him speaking to the heart. When every other voice is hushed, and in quietness we wait before Him, the silence of the soul makes more distinct the voice of God. He bids us, 'Be still, and know that I am God' Psalm 46:10. This is the effectual preparation for all labor for God.[8]

Our hearts need that quiet hour for communion. Put your phone on "do not disturb." Take time outside sitting in a peaceful place. Sit in the sanctuary alone. Linger in your car before moving towards your next meeting. Stop. Let your mind fill with God's goodness. Ask the Holy Spirit to guide you to a place of peace. Take a deep breath and let your body relax in the knowledge that "It is well with your soul." In this way, you will more deeply experience that God is God.

Being still in God's presence allows us to let go of the expectations that we have for ourselves and others. Being still in God's presence, we are able to release the persona, the mask, and the protection that we wear to safeguard ourselves. We realize we belong to God alone. We acknowledge that only God is God.

Prayers When We Have No Words

There are times when we have no words. When the loss is too raw and hasn't yet formed into a clear lament. When anger burns inside us. When God feels far away. In those times when you sit with God in prayer, recall the promise of Romans 8:26-27: "The Spirit helps us in our weakness… interceding for us with wordless groans." We don't need words in order to be understood. The whole range of our human experience is understood and known by God. Bring it all. Even if you have no words to yet express or make sense of it, bring it all. It's been particularly helpful for me to prayer journal in order to open up my mind and heart to God.

When we have no words, we can know this about how God receives us. Ellen White writes that our prayers, "may be inaudible to any human ear, but they cannot die away into silence, nor can they be lost through the activities of business that are going on. Nothing can drown the soul's desire. It rises above the din of the street, above the confusion of the multitude, to the heavenly courts. It is God to whom we are speaking, and our prayer is heard."[9] Know that God hears you and understands more than you can verbalize or make sense of.

The Face of God

Dallas Willard once wrote about a small child who crept into his father's bedroom to sleep. In the dark, knowing his father was present was enough to take away his sense of aloneness. "Is your face turned toward me, Father?" he would ask. "Yes," his father replied. "My face is turned towards you." Only then could he fall asleep.[10]

The night falls on us. There are times we don't know what's going on. We are not in control. We don't have the answers. A relationship with God does not take away the uncertainty, but in the darkness, we can ask, "God is your face turned towards me?" God responds to us, "Yes, My child. My face is turned towards you. My eyes are always on you."

God never stops, never quits, never fails to reach out to you, always available for a special, personal relationship. God who refuses to let death, darkness, chaos or pain have the last word in your life, the church, and the world. God is calling you and me to a relationship.

As Adventists, we believe that all life change starts with turning toward God, responding to this God who loves us first. Pray the Scriptures. Lift up your hands. Intercede for others. Use all your senses. Practice gratitude and praise. Be still. Trust that when you have no words, you are still deeply understood. You are invited to grow in a relationship with God.

> *May you experience the gift of God's presence in prayer, perhaps even trying new ways to pray.*
>
> *May you be honest and show up with God exactly as you are.*
>
> *May you know, no matter what, that God's face is turned towards you in love.*

Discussion Questions

1. What insight from the prayer life of Jesus most inspires you?
2. What is one new way to pray that you'd like to try this week?
3. What is one thing you can praise God for right now, regardless of your circumstances?

CHAPTER TWELVE

A Call to Rest: Sabbath Restoration

"It's not that we don't love God, it's that we don't know how to sit with God anymore."

A. J. SWOBODA

SOME YEARS AGO, the local newspapers in Tacoma, Washington, created a local hero when they reported the story of Tattoo, the basset hound.[1] Tattoo never intended to go for an evening run, but had no choice when his owner shut his leash in the car door and took off for a drive – with Tattoo outside the vehicle.

Police motorcycle officer, Terry Filbert, was driving near North 21st and Adam Street at about 7:25 PM, when he noticed a vehicle that appeared to have something dragging from it. As Filbert passed the vehicle, he saw the basset hound on a leash, "picking them up and putting them down as fast as he could."

Filbert pursued the car to a stop but not before the dog reached speeds in excess of 25 miles per hour and rolled over several times. The car's occupants, a man and a woman, jumped out when Filbert told them they were dragging a dog. The driver was distressed, shouting, "Tattoo, Tattoo!" The dog, eight months old, was uninjured and no citation was issued.

Ever feel like Tattoo—picking them up and putting them down as fast as you can? Racing through life? Yes, we can all relate. We face this challenge—a fixation with speed.

> *How did it get so late so soon?*
> *It's night before*
> *it's afternoon.*
> *December is here before it's June.*
> *My goodness how the*
> *time has flewn.*
> *How did it get so late so soon?*
> – THEODOR GEISEL [ALSO KNOWN AS DR. SEUSS]

How did it get to this pacing of go, go, go? How did it get so late so soon?

Yet, what we want is more meaning. A deeper and more fulfilling life.

Beyond physical rest. Beyond emotional rest. We are people in need of spiritual rest.

The need for rest—a deep kind of rest—was woven into us from the start. On the sixth day of creation, God made humans—men and women. The very next day was a day like no other. God did not create; instead, God celebrated with rest.

Our very first day as a human race was not about what we did, but who we were with! This tells us something of our purpose and our identity.

Seventh-day Adventists believe that our gracious God gave the gift of Sabbath rest to humanity at Creation. The Sabbath is God's enduring sign of the covenant of love God has made with humanity. The response to our need for deep rest. At our core we believe that God is on the throne and worthy of worship on the Sabbath. As the sun goes down on Friday, we are reminded of who we are and who we are not. We remember the God who loves us, created us, redeems us, and is with us.

In Genesis 2:1-3, right from the start, the cycle is set up. Work six days and rest on the seventh. Work on Sunday, Monday, Tuesday, Wednesday, Thursday, and Friday, but rest on Saturday, the seventh day of the week.

There is no creation without celebration. Work for six days, then enter into rest. The Sabbath is the highest point of creation. This word for rest isn't about relaxation alone. It has a full, rich meaning of entering into the fullness of life.

The verbs that are used here in the Hebrew are interesting. The format suggests that God was ceasing activity on the seventh day, but not only that. God was settling into the stability of the cosmos that had just been created. Experiencing refreshment by the security of what had been made, God blessed this space in time and extended favor to it.

Structurally, the climax of creation was rest. Communion. Ceasing. Relating. A deep breath and knowing that truly, "All is well." All the work is done, even if it isn't. God invites us to celebrate what has just happened and what continues to happen everyday in the world: the creative, benevolent power of God.

When we set aside time for rest, we acknowledge that all time is God's. As one commentator states, "We set aside the tyranny of the urgent and recapture the equilibrium that God established when he ordered the cosmos."[2]

Judith Shulemitz from the NY Times asks the question in a column about the Sabbath saying, "Why should God have considered it so important to stop?" For the answer she quotes Rabbi Elijah of Vilna saying, "God stopped to show us that what we create becomes meaningful to us only once we stop creating it and start to think about why we did so." Shulemitz goes on to summarize saying, "We have to remember to stop because we have to stop to remember."[3]

This is what it means to live aware of our humanity, honoring our Creator. There is a rhythm of work and rest. Work and celebration. Stop. Rest. See what God is doing. Take a day to make peace with what you can't control. Lay down your toiling and your controlling. Enter into rest. Break the spell that everything depends on you.

Ten Commandments

Seventh-day Adventists believe that this gift of Sabbath is a gift from God, given at creation as the birthright of humanity to live as a human being, not a human doing. The Ten Commandments protect every human relationship—with God, with our internal selves, and with each other. The Fourth Commandment says you need rest. You need rhythm. You need this cycle in which you stop and remember who God is and who you are.

I recently finished a book called *Thrive* by Arianna Huffington, founder of the Huffington Post. This book shares the importance of rest, sighting that we must end our delusion that burnout is the price we must pay for success. She advocates for sleep, making a difference, stillness, wholeness—all things needed to thrive. As I was listening to this audiobook, I looked up startled at hearing the Fourth Commandment being read. Arianna is spiritual but not religious, yet from her own life and her story of complete burnout, she discovered the importance of the Sabbath rest.

From Exodus 20:8-11, the command reads:

"Remember the Sabbath day by keeping it holy. Six days you

shall labor and do all your work, but the seventh day is a Sabbath to the LORD your God. On it you shall not do any work, neither you, nor your son or daughter, nor your manservant or maidservant, nor your animals, nor the alien within your gates. For in six days the LORD made the heavens and the earth, the sea, and all that is in them, but he rested on the seventh day. Therefore the LORD blessed the Sabbath day and made it holy."

So, God says, one seventh of all your time is to be devoted solely to relationships, with me and with other people. You and I need rest. Just as strongly as God commands that we not murder, or commit adultery or lie, God says Rest. Remember. Stop. Reflect. Maybe you were raised so strictly that all you hear when I mention the commandments is "thou shalt not." Growing up, that phrase eclipsed the meaning of the Sabbath. Maybe you feel constrained, frustrated, or waves of guilt all over again as you think of it. Or maybe you've been so focused on worshipping on the right day that it has been a long time since you let yourself rest in body, mind, and heart.

Remember this context: God gave this command in Exodus when the people were leaving slavery. Rescued from hundreds of years of oppression, God's people didn't know who they were anymore. They were slaves. Their worth was all based on how many bricks they could make. So interwoven all throughout the redemption and freedom story is the Sabbath. God was teaching the people again what it meant to be human, what it meant to be God's children. This is how you live: rest and then work. Back to the way you were designed at creation.

Liberation

God's voice speaks through the Sabbath: your worth and your value don't come from how many bricks you make, but because you are Mine. You are My child, My disciple, My beloved. Your worth and your value are not from what you do, but from the reality that you are Mine. Take one day per week to remind yourself that you are a person, not a machine. Take one day to be re-created. "I will be with you. I will give you rest," God promises.

In Genesis 2:3, it says that God blessed the Sabbath day. God made it holy, or set it aside for a different use. "Within the context of the Law, it means that the day belonged to God; it was for rest from ordinary labor, worship, and spiritual service. The day belonged to God."[4] This day had a different purpose than all the others.

Pastors are not exempt from this struggle with identity and where our worth comes from. The journey of practicing Sabbath has been an ongoing growth that has become richer and more meaningful for me over the years. For me, the practice of Sabbath means refusing to engage with certain questions or planning details on the Sabbath. It means preparing and then leaning into trust and the moving of the Holy Spirit for what God has prepared for us all. It means not connecting to social media and email for a set period of time in order to connect to God and who I am in God. It means turning off my phone or using "Do Not Disturb" at key times throughout the week. It means being conscientious of how I show up to the love of God and those around me. It means coloring in a coloring book with my son. It means noticing someone's expression and offering a hug. It means taking the time to pray for the people around me as we kneel in prayer, not just focusing on whatever is coming next. It means entering fully into worship. It means being in spaces and places where I can simply be. It's an ongoing journey.

Worship

The Pharisees not only focused on external behaviors such as Sabbath-keeping, but also seemed to trust in them, as if doing activities somehow made them holy (rather than God's making them holy). For Jesus, such practices were a means to an end: a way of connecting with God. For the Pharisees, the tools were the "end." Doing them was the point![5]

In the Gospel accounts, we see that Jesus lived a life with His eyes fixed on the right priorities. Jesus lived a life of Sabbath—work, then rest, work, then rest. Throughout His life, Jesus spent Sabbaths in the synagogue instructing people in the Scriptures; He spent time with His community—His friends; He spent time outdoors; and He spent time doing acts of mercy for others. These four things are activities that Jesus invites us to join in with Him.

Worship is the engagement of one's entire being with the greatness of the God who is. Worship is a life of conversation with God. God speaks, we respond, God responds, we respond again. Worship involves listening, looking, tasting, feeling, and smelling. We breathe in the presence of God wherever we are. We inhale the memories of faithful acts in the past and promises of love in the future. Just as we suffocate for lack of air, worship suffocates for lack of attentiveness to God's presence and faithfulness.

On the Sabbath, we are invited to the rest and restoration that comes as God's gift in worship. The gift of worship is our invitation every day as individual believers. Yet on the Sabbath day, the worshipping community gathers to worship God communally—truly a high day!

Dallas Willard wrote, "We dishonor God as much by fearing and avoiding pleasure as we do by dependence upon it or living for it."[6] (Of course, we are talking about godly, wholesome and healthy pleasure). What do children do when they celebrate? They make noise, lots of noise. There's nothing wrong with this, in the appropriate context and setting. Miriam the prophetess led the people in a great celebration dance. David went leaping and dancing before the Lord with all his might. You and I are invited to join in the celebration that comes as we experience rest.

Revelation 4 and 5 contain my favorite worship scenes in the

Scriptures—the ultimate worship. God is good and the life God gives us is good. The gathered host joins together to sing, bow down, and celebrate Jesus in their midst. This is true for us today. There is beauty to celebrate. There is love to celebrate. There are answers to prayer to celebrate. There are victories to celebrate. There are changed lives to celebrate. There is a wonderful future to celebrate. The Sabbath is a special time to celebrate and worship God.

A Called-Out People

We are called to be different. A people who stand out and who inspire others in the pacing of our lives. It is possible to be busy and not to be in a hurry. Busyness is a full life and can be lived with an attentiveness and dependence on God for each part. Hurrying crowds out our availability to God, giving our souls the sense of always rushing.

Perhaps what it looks like to live as called-out people is that we stop answering the question, "How are you?" with the word "busy." Perhaps we practice trust and letting go by stopping when Sabbath comes. At sundown, whether or not our work is done, we sit and enter into God's rest. Perhaps we lay down our worry, surrender our anxiety, and enter into worship. Perhaps we intentionally build in Sabbath practices that Jesus did: worship, community, rest, acts of mercy, and service.

What does this look like for you?

In music, the notes have meaning because of the rests, the pauses that allow us to be able to recognize the melody. In our lives, our activity has meaning because of the rest that we take. It is only through rest that what we do has any meaning at all. God offers us the greatest rest because it's not only physical rest; it's rest from trying to be all and do all in life. So often we leave our days feeling incomplete, inadequate, and run down. Sabbath reminds us that it's not about what we do, but who we are and who made us. "It's not how many bricks you make, My daughter, My son; it's because you're Mine," God says. It reminds me that it's not by what I do as a disciple of Jesus that I am made right with God or have meaning in my life. It's because of what Jesus has done.

God, the Creator of all, set up the Sabbath for us to be in a relationship—with God, with each other, and with all of creation. When we stop and honor this Sabbath that God made holy—set it aside as different than the other six days—we are acknowledging God as our Creator, as Master, and as the one who knows what is best for us.

In Matthew 11:28, 29, Jesus said, "Come to me, all you who are weary and burdened, and I will give you rest. Take my yoke upon you and learn from me, for I am gentle and humble in heart, and you will find rest for your souls."

This is what you were made for. Do you want to accept the Sabbath rest and all the beauty it holds? "It is for freedom that Christ has set us free" (Galatians 5:1). You were made for freedom! The Sabbath is a special date every week that God has set aside for you. You are invited into rest. You are invited to worship. You are invited to celebrate.

The Sabbath is inclusive (for all of us!), liberating (we are set free!), and healing (we remember who we are).

May you know that your worth and your value are not from what you do, but because you are God's child.

May you take one day per week to remind yourself you are a human being, not a human doing.

May you learn to practice the gift of Sabbath rest in your daily life as a disciple of Jesus.

Discussion Questions

1. What is one area of your life where you feel like you're just "picking them up and putting them down as fast as you can"?
2. What is one practical way you can enter more deeply into Sabbath rest?
3. What does it look like in your church to "set aside the tyranny of the urgent" and dedicate yourselves to living in the spirit of Sabbath?

CHAPTER THIRTEEN

A Call to Community: Life Together

"Encourage the expression of love toward God and toward one another. The reason why there are so many hardhearted men and women in the world is that true affection has been regarded as weakness, and has been discouraged and repressed."

ELLEN WHITE

RESEARCH SHOWS that deep and lasting loneliness has dire consequences for mental and physical health, increasing blood pressure and causing cardiovascular damage. Prolonged loneliness carries a higher morbidity risk than obesity, and some research indicates that it is as harmful as smoking 15 cigarettes a day.[1]

University of Chicago professor John Cacioppo says that the feeling of loneliness in the United States has doubled from 20% in the 1980s to 40% today.[2] Apparently, this uber-connected generation is . . . disconnected. Strange, isn't it, that our isolation is increasing in the time when we are more networked and connected than ever before.

At a horse-pull in Canada, one horse pulled 9,000 pounds, and another pulled 8,000 pounds. Together, we might assume that they could pull 17,000 pounds. However, when harnessed together these mighty steeds pulled 30,000 pounds, over three times what either could pull separately![3]

Similarly, God's power through the community of the church is greater than the sum of God's power in our lives individually. It's time to reconnect to the power of life lived in community.

For many years the church has encouraged believers to operate as if they were isolated from the world around them. Gallup states that "Americans are among the loneliest people in the world."[4] If we're honest, we find that the loneliness "out there" is also the loneliness inside the walls of the church, and inside us too.

Christianity has been plagued by years of individualizing the faith experience. The Seventh-day Adventist Church has not remained untouched by this focus. In recent decades, there has been a reawakening to the necessity of community in the discipleship process. Mega church pastor Keith Meyer has seen the power of spiritual transformation through seeking God in community. As studies began to show that mega churches were failing to produce changed lives, Meyer was one of those leaders who was willing to take the difficult challenge of assessing their approach and making corresponding changes to their church culture. They began the journey of connecting people in lasting community in new ways.[5]

Change that takes place in community is one of the most powerful and lasting. Henry Cloud and John Townsend point out that since humanity is wounded in community, God uses community to play a key part in healing those wounds.[6] The goal of the discipleship process in the local church is to experience transformation and healing together, experiencing mutuality in our shared journey.

Many people feel a hunger for something more in their church interactions.[7] Discipleship in community is a response to this need to *do life* together. Intentional discipleship brings "a layer of structure and intentionality to our otherwise random and unstructured friendships."[8] In the Adventist Church, during the formation of our denomination, small groups in homes, prayer bands, and more intimate sharing circles were common. These gave opportunity for deeper connection and depth among the believers. In addition, they made space for accountability and mentoring.

Accountability

An important aspect of discipleship and transformation through community is accountability. Accountability is often misunderstood. Cloud and Townsend assert that it is far more than just reporting your progress to others or having the experience of confessing to others that helps you bring about change in your personal life.[9] Healthy accountability is about disciples bringing their whole selves into the group (or community) and allowing the community to help with the growth and repair process that God is working in their individual lives. The group not only helps members to look at the external behavior, but also helps them plunge deeper into understanding the reasons behind what they are doing.

In the discipleship process, accountability is woven into the fabric of the process. It begins with the shared commitment to show up in each other's lives throughout the course of the discipleship journey (in the case of *Deep Calling*, a 12-week time period). Agreeing to ground rules for relationship and transparency in sharing, both set the stage for mutual accountability.

Mentoring

Walking with someone down a path that you have already been down and aiding in their journey is an apt metaphor for mentoring. Mentoring can be a useful tool for experiencing transformation through community. It can be done in the group setting or with just one individual and is the process of opening oneself to the input and wisdom of someone outside of oneself.[10]

We see this in the natural world. Cats don't know how to kill mice until they see it done. There are skills animals will not learn unless there is a more experienced adult to teach them. In the same way, there are things in our spiritual life that cannot be learned by reading or an online search. Spiritual maturity must be witnessed. As Paul said, follow my example (Philippians 3:17).

Mentoring in the discipleship process takes place primarily on the peer-to-peer level. The leader must not assume a mentor or "master" role with the group, but instead, facilitate space for the mutual mentoring that will take place within the group. Where one is strong, another may be weaker and vice versa. God knows how to match partners and groups in order to grow participants. The role of leaders is vital, and certainly they do serve as mentors in key moments; however, the weight of mentoring for the entire group does not rest on them.

The story is told of a man who was walking down the street when he fell into a pit in the ground. The walls were so steep that he couldn't get out. A doctor passed by and the guy shouted up, "Hey you. Can you help me out?" The doctor wrote a prescription, threw it down in the hole, and moved on. Then a pastor came along, and the man shouted up, "Pastor, I'm down in this hole. Can you help me out?" The pastor wrote out a prayer, threw it down in the hole, and moved on.

Then a friend walked by. "Hey, Joe, it's me, can you help me out?" The friend jumped in the hole. Our guy said, "Are you stupid?

Now we're both down here." The friend said, "Yeah, but I've been down here before and I know the way out."

The strength of community is that we each have experience, strength, and hope that we can lend to one another to lead the way out of wherever we've gotten stuck.

Community meets the needs of individual loneliness and isolation in this connection-deprived society, helping to restore the biblical paradigm for discipleship. Jesus set up an example in the way He called the first disciples to be with Him and with each other. It is this model that Jesus desires for the church. As Jesus stated in John 13:34-35, disciples are identified by the love they have for each other. People are able to see this love as disciples live in biblical community. In this complex world, biblical community in discipleship answers the longing of the human heart for companionship with God and fellow travelers.

Mission and Growth

A remarkable sense of community develops among disciples who are following Jesus together in mission. What binds the community of disciples together? First of all, as Dietrich Bonhoeffer points out, each disciple has experienced the forgiveness of their sins in Jesus Christ. It is this understanding of who they were before encountering Jesus, and who they are now in Jesus that characterizes the relationships between believers. All those gathered to Jesus know that without God, they are without hope. Together they stand on common ground as they recognize that they are sinners saved by grace (Ephesians 2:4-6; 1 Peter 2:9). Second, it is the shared commission to do Jesus' work in the world that unifies His people together (Matthew 28:18-20). God lives in the church (Ephesians 2:19-22) and is reconciling the world through God's people (2 Corinthians 5:17-21). This binds believers even more closely together as the body of Christ (1 Corinthians 12).

For the disciple, the life, death, and resurrection of Jesus changes how they interact with others. Notice that after Pentecost, the group of original disciples allowed Jesus to form their lives around their relationships with God and the people around them. Acts 2:46-47 describes, "Every day they continued to meet together in the temple courts. They broke bread in their homes and ate together with glad and sincere hearts, praising God and enjoying the favor of all the people. And the Lord added to their number daily those who were being saved." As they were united together with Jesus and each other, God was able to continue to add people to the church. Church growth is spoken of in relational terms—between God and the believer, as well as among the believers themselves.

As the church met, ate, praised, and enjoyed favor together, God was able to bring about growth. They met with glad and sincere hearts—an openhearted attitude, no performance. There was a generosity and devotion that characterized their time together. This kind of fellowship led to praise and to favor with others. The community they experienced led to expansion of the community.

Notice that there's not a single part of the life following Christ that you are meant to do alone. The entire Christian life is meant to be done in community. Meeting. Eating. Serving. Struggling. Growth. Unfortunately, we often miss the plural "you" in Greek. In our English Bibles, it looks like it's on us, "you," when we should understand it's all of us together. Maybe we need to use the Texan "y'all" or "all of you" in our Bibles. The life of devotion to Christ is meant to be lived out in community.

Not Without Challenges

This does not mean that community comes easily or quickly. Genuine community comes about as people follow Christ together, and it is not something that humans can fabricate themselves. Not unlike the salvation experience, community is a gift that only God can give.[11]

It is God who drives all aspects of authentic Christian community. The disciple's ongoing experience with Jesus' extravagant forgiveness slowly transforms them into a person who forgives others (Ephesians 4:31-32). The disciple's experience with God's consistent love changes them into a person who shares love with others (1 Corinthians 13:4-7). The way the disciple treats others is evidence of God's work in them. The outward fruit testifies to the inward transformation (Luke 6:43-45).

Why will spiritual transformation through an emphasis on discipleship make a more vibrant church culture? Disciples who have a living relationship with Jesus through which they are experiencing God's love, mercy, and joy bear this same fruit in their relationships with others. For example, many of the spiritual disciplines center around listening to God. By learning to listen to God, disciples learn to listen to those around them—both within and outside of the church. By listening more deeply to those around them, they are better able to reach them with the good news of Jesus and God's love for them. In communicating the love of Christ, disciples are accomplishing the mission.

It is the expression of Jesus' love in the life of the community that works to draw others into a relationship with Him (John 17:20-23). Jesus said that it is by love expressed to one another that people would be able to recognize the disciples of Jesus (John 13:34-35).

It is the love of Jesus that binds disciples together and prepares them for their work with Jesus in the world. Ellen White shares the winsome nature of this love in the following way:

> The knowledge of the Saviour's matchless love for them was to *bind them heart to heart,* preparing the way for the Lord to anoint them with his Spirit. United by this love, they were to go forth to witness with convincing power to the divinity of their Leader. And their Christlike love for one another was to be the sign of their discipleship.[12] (emphasis mine)

The Savior's love, unity in the church, and power in witnessing are all realized in the lives of the believers as they follow Jesus together on God's mission in the world. Out of this fusion comes the divine gift of community and sense of belonging for the believers.

Together

I got an unsolicited magazine in the mail. Paging through it before tossing it in the recycle bin, my eyes landed on this news, reported in May 2019.[13] The Scripps National Spelling Bee ran out of difficult words, and declared the final eight contestants co-champions, the most extraordinary ending in the event's 92-year history! The contestants all calmly went through the 20 final rounds, with words like:

> *sphaeriid* – sense organ found on the exterior of most sea urchins
>
> *huanglongbing* – a disease that prevents citrus fruit from ripening

Then, in a remarkable surprise, they were all declared the winners, the prestigious competition's first "octo-champions." This cost the organization $400,000 vs. $50,000 if there had been one winner!

We are living in an individualistic age—a time where we focus on what you as an individual can accomplish. This idea of more than one winner is so foreign. They've had a handful of other times where a tie between two winners occurred, but never more than two. Think of the investment these kids made. The kids have coaches, they practiced on a rigorous schedule, they invested their time, and sacrificed other sports and hobbies. And at the end of it all, there were eight winners. Some outsiders were upset, wondering how the organization could have failed to declare a winner. This flies in the face of the individualism we are so accustomed to.

The reaction of the kids? They were full of joy. Instead of representing the organization solo, they now got to travel and represent with other kids and they were elated.

Albert Schweitzer said, "In everyone's life, at some time, our inner fire goes out. It is then burst into flame by an encounter with another human being. We should all be thankful for those people who rekindle the inner spirit."[14]

They did it together. Not one winner, but eight. That's what I pray our life is like.

Beyond sharing the title at the spelling bee, the truth is we cannot do it alone. We weren't designed to do it alone. My prayer is that when the confetti falls at the end of life, you're surrounded, not by strangers you're competing against, but by friends who are supporting you.

I want to remind you that you aren't made to do life alone. Who are your people? How are you experiencing support from others? The best way you can make space for others to experience community and do life together in a discipleship group is if you are experiencing community in your own life.

Maybe for you that radical life lived in community will begin small today. Opening up to a friend about what you're really facing. Being vulnerable with a colleague. Forgiving someone who hurt you and caused you to shut down part of your heart to relationships with others. Recommitting to the living Word of God with a friend. This life together is compelling. This life together matters.

Remember, we saw in Acts 2 that it was the way they shared life which caused others to come their way and commit to Jesus. The numerical growth of the church was all from community, the quality of their fellowship. Imagine that! I believe it's the same vision of community that will meet the needs of the world we live in today.

> *May you experience the care and compassion, growth and guidance of God through community.*
>
> *May you have courage to show up, vulnerable and honest.*
>
> *May you relentlessly pursue structuring space for others to do life together.*

Discussion Questions

1. What is your church doing to be intentional about community outside of Sabbath mornings?
2. What is your church doing to encourage an atmosphere where everyone can win and celebrate together, not just individuals?
3. Who are the people who support you? How can you reach out to them and thank them?

CHAPTER FOURTEEN

A Call to Healing: Wholeness in Brokenness

"How sweet the name of Jesus sounds, in a believer's ear! It soothes his sorrows, heals his wounds, and drives away his fear."

JOHN NEWTON

SOMETIMES WE THINK what keeps us from fellowship with God and with each other is our pain and brokenness. We think of the things that we still do, say, and hold that we can't seem to get over. We think of the dreams and longings that we have that have gone unfulfilled. The words, actions, and circumstances of the past that prevent us from experiencing the forgiveness, healing, and mutual support of community.

Well, according to the follower and friend of Jesus who wrote the letter we are about to read in part, what keeps us from the light of God (i.e. in our darkness) is our unwillingness to admit the truth. It's our claiming what is not, instead of owning the truth.

"This is the message we have heard from him and declare to you: God is light; in him there is no darkness at all. If we claim to have fellowship with him and yet walk in the darkness, we lie and do not live out the truth. But if we walk in the light, as he is in the light, we have fellowship with one another, and the blood of Jesus, his Son, purifies us from all sin" (1 John 1:5-7).

Lying to ourselves, to God, and to each other keeps us in the darkness and out of the light. It's not our brokenness or our pain; it's our resistance to being honest about that pain. Merriam-Webster's Dictionary defines lying as "to create a false or misleading impression." In the words of John, we are claiming something, yet doing another thing all together.

The truth is that we sometimes don't like who or what we are so we try to make it seem that we're something we're not. It is this game of charades, costumes, and cover that keeps us from experiencing the beauty, the joy, the freedom that comes from walking in the light of God's healing. As Kathleen Norris says, "We want life to have meaning, and want to be fulfilled, and it is hard to accept that we find these things by starting where we are, not where we would like to be."[1]

This call of God to healing is an invitation to start where we are—right in our mess, in our unwillingness to forgive… in our bitterness… in our jealousy… in our pain… in our unbelief… in the way we just can't seem to move on. In this place of honesty, we find that Jesus whispers, "If we confess our sins, he is faithful and just and will forgive us our sins and purify us from all unrighteousness" (1 John 1:9). We hear, "By His wounds, we are healed" (1 Peter 2:24). This promised healing is for all of us, for you and for me.

Come into the light of authenticity. I believe we will find that healing, freedom, forgiveness, fellowship, and grace all begin with being honest with God, ourselves, and others about where we are right now. There is a newness of life for us. By walking in the light of God, we are willing to say what areas of our lives need healing and to reach after God who desires to make us whole. Like the man at the pool, Jesus asks us, "Do you want to be healed?" (John 5:6, ESV). God desires to make you whole in body, mind, and heart (Psalm 147:3).

Discipleship and Healing

The discipleship journey must, by necessity, involve growing in emotional and spiritual health. We are whole beings. As the disciple grows up in God, wounds of the heart and mind are exposed, faced, and healed. God brings a fuller life to the followers, and rather than this spiritual growth disconnecting the disciples from life, the disciples become healthier in their connection with all of life. Benner exhorts that becoming "more spiritual" must be grounded in becoming "more human." He continues, "If embracing humanness was good enough for Jesus, how can we despise it? To become like Jesus and take on his character, we must—like Him—embrace our humanity and work out our spirituality within it."[2]

The emphasis on transformation through emotional healing developed in Christian culture during the last few decades. David Seamands was one of the key pioneers in connecting emotions and the spiritual life, as were Henry Cloud and John Townsend.[3] As a minister, Seamands describes his experience of working with people with problems that were not being healed by prayer and faithful practice of the spiritual disciplines alone.[4] I've observed this in my own ministry, and other authors have written on the same theme.[5] Pete Scazzero hit a wall in his own life and ministry and came to the realization that "emotional health and spiritual maturity are inseparable."[6]

My journey has been strengthened by Scazzero, Seamands, and Cloud and Townsend, as they have shown their personal experiences with emotional healing and the value of the interior work in that process. We do not need to choose God or counseling. There is a role for counselors, psychologists, and other therapists in the work of healing. Some find themselves resistant to supportive therapies that would benefit them, especially when coupled with healing work done in and through the body of Christ. Healing in community is one of the gifts God works through with God's people.

In the dozens of times I have gone through the discipleship journey *Deep Calling* with groups, I have witnessed how God has worked miracles of emotional healing in participants' lives in the process of seeking God in a community of believers. I have observed that both the supernatural work of God and human psychological support (through peers) are essential for emotional healing. There have been times when issues were raised in the discipleship journey that allowed participants to be freed from a burden of guilt, pain, or shame they had been carrying since childhood. There were other times when the discipleship journey led a participant to seek a referral for deeper work with a Christian counselor.

As a leader, it is essential to take a wholistic approach to discipleship. God desires to grow the disciple spiritually, emotionally, physically, mentally, and socially. While we may be unaware of the areas where God desires to work with a participant, we can pray for and support them on the journey on which God is leading them. We can encourage them towards greater emotional health because spiritual and emotional health are intrinsically connected. This support means that we stay open to the healing God may choose to work in a participant's life during the discipleship process, knowing that the Holy Spirit moves in the community and in the leader. This support also means we encourage ongoing work and stand ready with a Christian counselor referral, should one be desired.

In the discipleship journey, participants commit to focusing on Christ. In the midst is a parallel call to honesty and transparency with Christ and the community of believers. Emotional health and healing can only take place when believers approach Christ as they are. Instead of compartmentalizing faith into one of the categories of life, discipleship is a call to surrender the entire life to Jesus, even emotional healing, and to face that process with honesty. This surrender is best done with the support of Christian community.

Discipleship and Suffering

Many times, believers are not taught that part of the spiritual journey is accepting conflict and suffering in life. Consciously or unconsciously, when people accept Christ, many expect that everything will get easy for them. The stories in the Bible contradict this expectation. As we see in the Scriptures, challenges and trials came *because* individuals were making the decision to follow Christ. As Russell Burrill shares, "One who becomes a disciple of Jesus can be expected to be treated as Jesus was treated—misunderstood and persecuted."[8] It is a challenge to face even the everyday troubles that are simply a part of being alive, let alone the direct hardships that come as a result of commitment to following Jesus.[9]

Far from becoming easier upon accepting Christ, life can get harder. Pete Scazzero points out that "Job was innocent. There was no connection between his sin and the amount of pain he experienced. This seems terribly unfair."[10] Unfair and difficult to accept, but true. Scazzero again emphasizes, "The heart of Christianity is that the way to life is through death, the pathway to resurrection is through crucifixion."[11] He also adds a word of caution: "Remember, resurrection only comes out of death—real death. Our losses are real."[12] Disciples must humbly come face to face with struggle, loss, and hardship—to die—before they can experience resurrection. This is one of the paradoxes of the Christian life: to find your life you must first lose it.

As a person who went through suffering in the name of God and because of his convictions, Bonhoeffer appeals to us:

> If we refuse to take up our cross and submit to suffering and

rejection . . . we forfeit our fellowship with Christ and have ceased to follow Him. But if we lose our lives in His service and carry our cross, we shall find our lives. . . . Discipleship means allegiance to the suffering Christ.[13]

Discipleship is a calling to experience a wide-ranging connection with Christ—participating in Jesus' resurrection and abundant life, as well as His sufferings. Part of the discipleship journey must develop a maturity in participants that is able to bear the weight of disappointment, loss, and pain. Disappointment with "the church" and fellow Christians, loss that life brings, and pain over things they cannot control. When heartache comes and persecution brings anxiety, is there a relationship with God and the disciple that is able to withstand the weight of real experience?

Grasping the relationship between discipleship and suffering requires a serious paradigm shift. It comes down to understanding the reality that God uses suffering in the discipleship process. Bonhoeffer affirms that there is a cost—spiritually, mentally, physically, and emotionally—to following Christ completely. It means that Jesus takes center stage and first priority in everything, which can sometimes cause hardship.[14] Jim Cymbala adds perspective: "Trouble is one of God's great servants because it reminds us how much we continually need the Lord. Otherwise, we tend to forget about entreating him."[15]

We are to center on Jesus, looking for God in any and every situation and realizing, as Reggie McNeal maintains, that discipleship is "heart-shaping" which sometimes happens by trial.[16] As disciples are shaped by God through any and all circumstances, they seek to develop awareness of the mysterious ways God is forming them, especially through suffering. In the midst of this suffering, disciples continue to seek God who desires their healing.

Healing the World

Jewish tradition understands our job in this world as *Tikkun olam*. The common understanding of *Tikkun olam* is that we share in partnership with God in the repairing of the world.[17] With God and each other, we boldly take steps to help one another and bring honor to God. This Jewish concept encapsulates the understanding that we aren't just here for ourselves, but for the healing of one another and this earth. God is Healer. As children of the Creator, we are also healers.

Aware of the anguish facing those in our communities and our world, we set about our work of kindness, affirming the dignity of each human being. We set about our work of love, building bridges and connections between people. We set about our work of justice, righting wrongs and giving voice to the voiceless. As Bishop Leontine Kelly said, "healing has twin aspects; restoration now and empowerment for the future."[18] Our role in *Tikkun olam* is on behalf of one another, working for individuals as well as facing systems that threaten to overtake those most vulnerable.

People often ask me, why doesn't God just ditch this old earth, give up on humanity, start over? My answer is this: our God is Healer, a God of redemption, restoration, and wholeness. Our God delights in taking brokenness, misery and the wounded and transforming all to joy.

In Matthew 21:12-17, Jesus drove the moneychangers and salespeople out of the temple. To all those trying to make a profit off of the spiritual seekers, Jesus said, "My house is to be a house of prayer." Notice that immediately after Jesus clears out those who were distracting from worship, then the lame, the blind, the weak, and the wounded flock to Him, and He heals them. As soon as the religious distractions are driven away, healing takes place.

There are people around us carrying unspeakable pain—physical, spiritual, mental, and emotional pain that threatens to overcome them. Those bearing scars of abuse and injustice, depression and suicidal thoughts, hopelessness and isolation are invited to come and be near Jesus. This passage gives me great courage. As I am willing to allow Jesus to clear space in my life and my spiritual experience, it is there I find healing. As I own my own feebleness, blindness, and weakness, and come to Jesus, in that place I am made whole.

Driving out the distractions makes way for worship from children and healing for those who desperately need a Savior. Could the same be true today? Will we be a part of making space for the healing of God today? We are called to take up the burden of *Tikkun olam* and join God in the healing of the world around us.

Avenues of Healing

In what ways have you experienced the healing touch of God in your own life? The primary avenue of healing God has used in my life has been relationships. In timely conversations, heartfelt prayer sessions, and even during an anointing, I have experienced a healing balm for my soul.

Dianne Nue, Co-Director for the Women's Alliance for Theology, Ethics and Ritual encourages us to expand our view of how we receive healing from God:

> Healing takes many forms – from swallowing grandma's home remedies to having your scalp massaged and shampooed, from receiving a reconciling embrace to sobbing alone. We find healing through a sympathetic listener, a forgiving hug, a crying spell, a belly laugh, an herbal bath, a quiet time with nature, a moving sermon, a powerful Eucharist or a deeply meaningful ritual.[19]

Yes, it's all healing. All avenues for the grace of God in your life and in mine.

In God We Trust

As I sit, composing sentences for this chapter on healing, I receive a text from a friend that the cancer we had hoped was contained has indeed spread. It's a grounding reality. Even as we pray, we have no guarantee. Even as we seek healing, we don't know how or in what form that healing will come.

I've been a part of many anointings where the person received complete and total physical healing. I've been a part of numerous anointings where the healing was not physical and the answer we sought didn't come in the way we desired. I've been shaped by my time at the bedside. As we have buried beloved church members, as we lost my dad and my husband's mom to cancer, and as my own body ached in miscarriage, I have learned something about the sacred, healing power of God.

Dear friends, in light of all that we bring and all the healing we need, let us join in prayer at the close of this chapter. Bring whatever burdens your heart and the healing you long for. Let's pray:

God of all Healing, we trust in you.

We don't trust in having it all figured out.

We don't trust in knowing what to do.

We don't trust in having answers to our deepest questions

We realize that…

Even as we know God honors our faith, someone else finds out their child has cancer.

Even as one person starts work in their dream job, someone else goes through bankruptcy.

Even as someone feels healthier than they've ever been, someone else suffers a debilitating heart attack.

Even as one person feels connected in meaningful community, someone else feels isolated and all alone.

We can pray, but someone will still learn their loved one died in a car accident.

We can learn to right wrongs, but someone will still be treated unfairly based on their gender, race, or sexuality.

We can give, but we know it will never be enough.

We do not hope in what we can do, but in the power of God's love and healing to restore the world, both now, and in the blessed day that is coming. We bring everything that is hurting, all that is unfinished, all that grieves our hearts. We hear your words, to press near to the throne of grace. "Draw near and find help in your time of need" (Hebrews 4:16).

Oh God, this is our time of need.

When we are honest about the pain… When we are honest about our brokenness and the brokenness that is around us, it threatens to overwhelm us.

We turn to you, healing God.

Help us to hold tenaciously to hope, and when we cannot hope, may we realize Hope is holding onto us.

Heal us, Oh God, and may we be a part of bringing healing in this world.

Remind us that we live not by certainty, but by trust.

In the blessed and healing name of Jesus, Amen.

May you have courage to face the brokenness and pain in you and bring it to God and safe friends in honesty.

May you trust God's healing and pay attention to the avenues of healing God uses in your life.

May you be a channel of healing in this world.

Discussion Questions

1. In your journey towards healing, what is one area of brokenness God is inviting you to be more honest about?
2. Where in your church is there a need to see the connection between emotional and spiritual health?
3. What can you do to join God in the healing of the world around us?

CHAPTER FIFTEEN

A Call to Witness: Tell Your Story

"My prayer is that the Holy Spirit would sweep into our lives with holy disruption, upending our assumptions and privileges, our greed and selfishness, our pride and our stupor. To empower our work and our witness. Like Zechariah 4:6 tells us, not by might, not by power, but by my Spirit, says the Lord."

SARAH BESSEY

AS A CHILD, I READ BOOKS about Pippi Longstocking, a red-haired, freckle-faced fictitious girl who was spunky and strong. In the book, *Pippi Goes Aboard*, author Astrid Lindgren spins a tale that starts at the perfume shop window. In the shop window was a large jar of freckle salve, and beside the jar was a sign, which read: DO YOU SUFFER FROM FRECKLES?

"What does the sign say?" asked Pippi Longstocking. She couldn't read very well because she didn't want to go to school as other children did.

"It says, 'Do you suffer from freckles?'" said Annika.

"Does it indeed?" said Pippi thoughtfully. "Well, a civil question deserves a civil answer. Let's go in." She opened the door and entered the shop, closely followed by Tommy and Annika. An elderly lady stood back of the counter. Pippi went right up to her. "No!" she said decidedly.

"What is it you want?" asked the lady.

"No," said Pippi once more.

"I don't understand what you mean," said the lady.

"No, I don't suffer from freckles," said Pippi.

Then the lady understood, but she took one look at Pippi and burst out, "But, my dear child, your whole face is covered with freckles!"

"I know it," said Pippi, "but I don't suffer from them. I love them. Good morning."

She turned to leave, but when she got to the door she looked back and cried, "But if you should happen to get in any salve that gives people more freckles, then you can send me seven or eight jars."

If only we could be more like Pippi as we come into greater acceptance of who we are and the witness that we are called to have in the world.

Understanding of Self

As Christians center our lives on a relationship with Jesus through practice of the eight calls (the devotional practices) as a way of connecting with God, weaknesses and strengths will become apparent in ways not experienced before. We may discover that we have difficulty practicing one of the devotional habits, or that one habit comes far more easily and is desired more deeply than the rest. In the process of coming closer to Christ, disciples understand ourselves more deeply, and as we understand ourselves more deeply, we find a deeper understanding of Christ.

In his work using the Myers-Briggs Type Indicator (MBTI), Malcolm Goldsmith asserts that the better you understand yourself, specifically through the use of the personality types, the deeper your understanding of God. He uses the MBTI personality test to help individuals make sense of who they are and how to relate to God by way of the spiritual disciplines.

Dan R. Dick and Barbara Miller also make use of a Spiritual Gifts Inventory, which helps identify primary and secondary gifts from a list of 20 spiritual gifts derived from Scripture and early Christian writings. Through this process of knowing ourselves and how God wants to use us in the church and in the world, we disciples of Jesus are better able to grasp where to serve, how to work, and our unique way of responding to others, which depends on our relationship with God.

A commitment to honesty in coming to God is essential. Harri Kuhalampi shares his perspective on Ellen White's view of the wholistic nature of spirituality and sheds light onto the interplay between one's relationship with God and awareness of oneself. While defining prayer as "the opening of the heart to God as to a friend" she, White, expresses in a revealing way the essence of what Christian spirituality is all about:

> Being undisguised in the presence of God, facing him openly and candidly. Whatever is within is confronted with the full awareness that God sees all: feelings, memories, ideas, intentions, motive, attitudes, relationships, experiences, etc. A person of this attitude must also be honest to the self and face all aspects of one's experience and inner life as well as every feature of one's personality and character.

To pursue Christ with "all your heart and with all your soul and with all your strength," as God invites believers in Deuteronomy 6:5, necessitates increasing awareness of all aspects of the self, including personality, spiritual gifts, and learning style. It is this increased understanding that profoundly influences how people relate to God, mission, community, and suffering. Our life's witness comes from the depth of our understanding of who we are and our story.

What happens after Jesus is the center of our lives as believers? J.P. Moreland notes that the problem of contemporary culture and the contemporary church is boredom. The remedy he suggests is a call for disciples to live in the drama—the "historic struggle between God's kingdom and all who oppose it." God's people are called for a purpose and it is in living out that purpose that we find ultimate fulfillment. In his classic, *The Purpose Driven Life,* Rick Warren adds that great purpose is discovered when we realize that this life, ultimately, is not about us.

Seth Godin simply states, "People seek meaning. Will you offer it to them?" We realize the emptiness of what we are involved in and long to be a part of something bigger than ourselves. People are asking the question Rick Warren frames, "What on Earth am I here for?" In other words, we want a mission and purpose beyond ourselves. We perceive the self-serving emphasis of our lives, and sense that true happiness only comes from living out our God-given purpose. People not only want a mission, but have been hard-wired for a mission (see Ephesians 2:10).

The life of a disciple stands in stark contrast to the self-serving life to which the secular world calls people. This life centers on the individual's goals, ambitions, dreams, and future. Instead, disciples of Jesus are compelled to live for the sake of others. Dallas Willard says, "We also need to keep in mind the multitudes of people (surrounded by churches) who will *not* be in heaven because they have never, to their knowledge, seen the reality of Christ in a living human being." In a similar vein, Rick Stearns, former President of

World Vision shares, "It is not our fault that people are poor, but it is our responsibility to do something about it. God says that we are guilty if we allow people to remain deprived when we have the means to help them."

Some readers may challenge this viewpoint, insisting that the thing that makes Christians unique is their belief in God, and not the action they take in the world. Others insist that the emphasis be placed on the way that Christians live—the outward changes of behavior that make them different from the rest of the world. Jan Paulsen calls this a tension between "cerebral" and "practical" Christianity. Christianity has become divided over which emphasis should have primacy: belief or what is done based on that belief. This is true in the Adventist Church as well.

We are called to reintegrate faith and works in the practice of our faith. In other words, the *being* and the *doing* of Christianity cannot be divided. Rick Stearns says it well: "This does not mean we are saved by piling up enough good works to satisfy God. No, it means that any authentic and genuine commitment to Christ will be accompanied by demonstrable evidence of a transformed life." Beliefs and actions are inseparable in discipleship. The good news of the gospel must be shared in word *and* deed, that is, our witness.

Most often, this expression of the gospel in word and deed is called evangelism and service. Foster, in outlining the six traditions of the Christian faith, refers to these as the Evangelical Tradition and the Social Justice Tradition. In this chapter, we will look at the call to witness through our lives, sharing the good news through evangelism. In the next chapter, we will look at the call to service. These aspects of the mission of Christ are those which captivate the heart's longing to make a difference in the world. First, our witness.

Evangelism

When it comes to evangelism, many think of big auditoriums, long appeal songs, and polished speakers. Humphrey and Humphrey challenge this picture and affirm that all are called to present the gospel through their everyday lives. In what is often called the faith chapter, Hebrews 11 shares a list of several of God's servants throughout time who utilized faith to make a difference in the world. The authors point out that of the names on that list, all but two were laypeople, not *professional* ministers. God's calling, they emphasize, is for *every* disciple of Christ to share the good news. McLaren defines evangelism by saying, "God's people are blessed *instrumentally* – blessed in order to be a blessing to *others* . . . *evangelism* means 'spreading good news.'"

Russell Burrill takes it one step further: "The Christian who is not reproducing by creating other disciples is not really a disciple. It is impossible . . . to be a follower of Jesus and not share Jesus." There is a clear imperative in Scripture for disciples to allow God to use them to make other disciples. The process of discipleship must emphasize the necessity of sharing the good news through everyday living, as well as partnering with God in the formation of other disciples. Imagine what it would be like if every disciple (each member) understood the importance of their role in the ministry and mission of Christ to bring the gospel to the world and lived out that mission? Jesus is waiting to do this through His disciples now.

Through our witness, our story, and our very lives, God wants to make the invisible Kingdom of God visible in the world today.

What does witness to the Kingdom of God look like? How is evangelism—sharing the good news—evidenced in our day-to-day lives?

Giving witness to the Kingdom is seen in the small decisions we make each day. It's when you stop to genuinely thank the people bagging your groceries, opening the door for you, or swiping your credit card. When you look them in the eye and wish them a good day. It's when your child interrupts you for the 10th time and you take a deep breath, stop, give them your full attention, and hear what they have to say, showing genuine interest, love, and care. It's when you are coming into church and you see a neighbor or passer-by on the street and you stop to say hello, ask them how they are doing, and wish them a good day. It's when you're in a hurry and you could just toss the glass jars of mostly used-up spaghetti sauce in the garbage, but instead, you choose to rinse them out and recycle them. It's when you're in the store and you see what you want there before you. You don't need it, but you want it. Instead of getting it, you walk away, knowing your happiness is not caught up in what you own and instead, you decide to give your money to ministry.

Giving witness to the Kingdom is seen in the larger decisions, the ones that take more sacrifice and intentionality with our time. It's when someone opens up to you about their struggles and you stop to hear their story. It's when you offer to give someone a Bible study and commit to meeting with them most every week, spending time together in the Word of God. It's when you courageously, bravely share your story, even the hard parts. When you share this testimony, you give others hope for what God can do in their lives. It's when you notice the people who are always silently working, never asking for much. You decide to pay attention to them and let them know you care to invest in their success. It's when you go to the assisted-living home, sing hymns and invite the staff to join you in choosing their favorites. It's when you share a spiritual book with your neighbor that talks about the very thing they mentioned they are going through. It's when you have the courage and relationship built to invite your co-worker to your church for a special program. Knowing they've been looking for a deeper experience with God, you serve as a bridge to connect them with the community of Christ.

In the Kingdom of God, we realize how short our lives are here, but that this isn't all there is. We want our lives and our witness to matter in the areas that will last for eternity. So, we invest, give, and prayerfully discern what matters and give all that we have to it in the witness of our lives. The truth is that the people of God, the church, is the plan of the Holy Spirit to make God's Kingdom visible. We give witness to the already inaugurated kingdom of God that began in Jesus Christ and now continues with each one of us.

God-Given Vision

Acts 9 begins with drama and intensity. Saul was breathing murderous threats against the followers of "the Way." So hot was his rage, that he requested permission to travel outside of Jerusalem to find those believers who may have fled. On the way, Jesus Himself spoke to him. In a flash of light from heaven, everything changed for Saul. He heard the voice, and as he discovered it was Jesus who was speaking to him, he also found out he was blind.

His companions led him into the city, where he fasted for 3 days in complete darkness. Why did God need to blind Saul for these days before he could receive his mission? Verse 15 declares God's purposes for Saul when it says, "This man is my chosen instrument to carry my name before the Gentiles and their kings and before the people of Israel." So, why did Saul sit in darkness? Sometimes in order to gain a new view of the future—a new calling, a new mission, a new witness—we need to sit in the dark for awhile. We need to have everything else removed from our sight. We must come to realize our need for direction, for guidance.

Into this void in Saul's life, God sent His servant Ananias to speak His plan and Saul received vision—physically and spiritually. Verse 18 says, "Immediately, something like scales fell from Saul's eyes, and he could see again. He got up and was baptized."

Whether you're joyfully fulfilling God's purpose for you each day, or waiting in the darkness for God's plan to be spoken into your life, or somewhere in between, know that God's desire is to direct you to make a difference for God's Kingdom, to live as a witness of God's goodness in the world. Sometimes that means we sit in darkness awhile before we receive our sight. These times can be hard, even challenging and confusing, but they also strengthen and grow us. Sit with the darkness. Trust God, who is constantly being revealed to you, for God will give you your sight. **The longing of God's heart is to give you and me vision and purpose, empowering us to witness to God's presence in the world with our very lives.**

Seek to discover more of who you are—your gifts, temperament, and personality. Understand your own story and how God has worked for your redemption. Openly share your story, bearing witness to the presence of God in your life. Reflect God in your decisions, both small and great. As you do, trust that God will give you an unfolding vision and a purpose beyond yourself.

> *May you realize God delights in who you are and designed you to be a unique witness in the world.*
>
> *May you witness to the Kingdom of God in our present lives by how you share with vulnerability, courage, and love.*
>
> *May you set out on the life-long quest, discovering more of who you are and God's purpose for your life.*

Discussion Questions

1. In what ways has understanding yourself more deeply helped you understand God more deeply?
2. What small decision can you make today to give witness to the Kingdom of God?
3. What part of Saul's story do you relate to the most? How can you share that part of your story with someone this week?

CHAPTER SIXTEEN

A Call to Serve: Incarnation

"A kind, courteous Christian is the most powerful argument that can be produced in favor of Christianity."

ELLEN WHITE

AS A TEENAGER, I loved "Magic Eye" books. Have you ever seen these books or posters? The books feature autostereograms, images which allow some people to see 3D images by focusing on the 2D pattern. For many people, bringing the book or image close to their eyes relaxes their vision enough so that when they pull it back, they are able to see the hidden picture. Something that was invisible moments before, suddenly becomes visible.

Disciples of Jesus make visible the invisible Kingdom of God through our witness and our service. Miraculously, something that was not visible—love, hope, or courage—is made visible through the life of the disciple. As Jesus did, the love of God is incarnate in our lives, being expressed day by day. As a church, we tend to separate the call to witness and the call to serve, as if some believers are called to evangelism, and others are called to service. While we all have different gifts, the calling of God to every disciple is both to witness through our life story and to serve those in need. The previous chapter focused on our witness. This chapter will focus on the call to service.

In his paraphrase of Matthew 25, Stearns encapsulates the call of Christ to serve the least of these.

> For I was hungry, while you had all you needed. I was thirsty, but you drank bottled water. I was a stranger, and you wanted me deported. I needed clothes, but you needed more clothes. I was sick, and you pointed out the behaviors that led to my sickness. I was in prison, and you said I was getting what I deserved.[1]

As our hearts are being transformed by a relationship with Christ, we can no longer view the world, or the suffering ones of the world, in the same way. Shane Claiborne is a leader of an intentional community re-imagining how Christians can respond to those with the greatest needs. He says they are creating "a community of people who have fallen desperately in love with God and with suffering people, and who allow those relationships to disturb and transform them."[2] It is this service, no matter how disturbing and difficult, that is the mission given to believers by Christ. Stearns calls this tenacious focus on service "The Whole Gospel," good news for the world that is wholistic in its reach.[3]

It is important for individual Christians, and the Christian community, to be aware of the hardship, poverty, and sickness that plagues the world, and to join together to make a difference. This is an essential part of spiritual life and growth. By serving, the disciple takes on the heart of Christ. Ellen White says that as servants of God become more like Jesus, they receive "the Spirit of Christ—the Spirit of unselfish love and labor for others." She concludes, "Your love [will] be made perfect. More and more you will reflect the likeness of Christ in all that is pure, noble, and lovely."[4] Transformation happens in the disciple as they pray for their heart to break for the people and issues that break the heart of God. Through service and prayer, the disciple is changed by the Jesus seen in the suffering ones.

A Divine-Human Partnership

Central to the message and mission of Jesus is the idea that God desires humans to partner in the redemptive work of God to the whole world. Matthew 28:18-20 shares the final words of Jesus to the disciples before He ascended into heaven. Jesus said:

> All authority in heaven and on earth has been given to me. Therefore, go and make disciples of all nations, baptizing them in the name of the Father and of the Son and of the Holy Spirit, and teaching them to obey everything I have commanded you. And surely, I am with you always, to the very end of the age.

These authoritative words from Jesus commission the disciples to go, make disciples, baptize, and teach all people to follow the way Jesus had taught them. The original disciples' willingness to heed these words is the reason there are disciples of Jesus today. At the heart of discipleship is following Jesus (Luke 9:23) and showing others what it looks like to follow Him (Acts 1:8), thereby having an active role in making new disciples of Jesus.

This same invitation has been a part of God's plan for humanity from the very beginning. From the creation of the world, God designed the human pair to cultivate and care for the world—land and animals alike. God brought humans into the process of tending what had been made, thus making them partners with Divinity. They fell, but through the sacrifice of Jesus, humanity has been made right with God again. "For if, by the trespass of the one man, death reigned through that one man, how much more will those who receive God's abundant provision of grace and of the gift of righteousness *reign* in life through the one man, Jesus Christ!" (Romans 5:17, emphasis added). Through the gift of grace in Jesus Christ, humans are once again able to be partners with Divinity. God invites each person to be a disciple, to be a part of this amazing, redemptive work in the world.

God never intended to stop being incarnate in the flesh – God just passed it on to the disciples, and now to us. God is now incarnate in you and me. To be incarnate is to touch and be touchable, to serve and to be served. This is what is modeled in the life of Jesus. The picture of God incarnate in us is compelling. God wants to do beyond what we are asking or yet imagining to make a difference in the world through us—the people of God. God wants to do something beautiful with the church, dwelling in us as we are reachable, touchable, and vulnerable to serve those around us.

In her book *Take This Bread*, Sara Miles shares that serving "doesn't promise to solve or erase suffering but to transform it, pledging that by loving one another, even through pain, we will find more life. And it insists that by opening ourselves to strangers, the despised or frightening or unintelligible other, we will see more and more of the holy, since, without exception, all people are one body: God's."[5] All of us are God's children.

In everything Jesus did, He was giving a living illustration to His followers so that they would learn how to do what He was doing. After Jesus washed the disciple's feet in service and humility, He said, "I have set you an example that you should do as I have done for you" (John 13:15). Disciples are called to do the same: inviting people to surrender to the Lordship of Christ as expressed in the Scriptures and showing them what that looks like with their own lives, just as Jesus did (Mark 10:35-45; John 13:35).

Learned Helplessness

Martin Seligman experimented at the University of Pennsylvania in the 1960's and first observed learned helplessness when he was doing experiments on dogs. Learned helplessness occurs when people or animals feel helpless to avoid negative situations. He noticed that the dogs didn't try to escape the shocks if they had been conditioned to believe that they couldn't escape.[6]

What does this mean for us? We can look at the darkness, look at the challenge, hear the bad news and actually believe that there is nothing we can do about it. We can look at homelessness, poverty, young people without mentors, hungry children, the effects of natural disasters, depressed friends, and struggling relationships and we can mistakenly believe that there is nothing we can do about it. We can begin to subconsciously live out the lie that the darkness overcomes the light, that the kingdom of this world is more powerful than the Kingdom of God.

We must reverse learned helplessness. God's Kingdom has come near. Right here, right now, even in the midst of these challenges, our compassionate actions on behalf of someone else is what makes the invisible kingdom visible. As Dale Carnegie said, "Most of the important things in the world have been accomplished by people who have kept on trying when there seemed to be no hope at all."[7] We, the disciples of Jesus, of all people should be the ones who persist in hope with the problems facing our neighbors.

What are the biggest problems facing the church? What are the biggest problems facing our community?

What can we do about these problems that face our churches and communities? How can light show up in small ways through us? How can the Kingdom of God come close? Let me tell you, I long for justice. I long for healing. I long for a world where there is no more death, sorrow, tears, or mourning. I long for things to be made whole again. What I find again and again is that the Spirit of God takes my longing and moves me to take action on behalf of someone else. To bring hope in seemingly hopeless situations. It never feels like enough, but it is something. I may not be able to visit everyone, but I can visit one. I may not be able to feed everyone, but I can feed this one. I may not be able to give to all, but I can give to this one.

The Spirit uses our longing and moves through us to take tangible actions which makes the hope in the ultimate fulfillment of our longing feel even closer. Even as the King is coming, the Kingdom of heaven is near (Matthew 4:17). As Dallas Willard said, "The gospel is less about how to get into the Kingdom of Heaven after you die, and more about how to live in the Kingdom of Heaven before you die."[8] Many small acts make the kingdom of God visible. Imagine a world where everyone said, I'm going to bring the kingdom near in my life. I'm going to make the invisible kingdom visible in what I say and do. Imagine if everyone said, "I'm going to invest in the wellbeing of another—bringing light to the darkness right here, right now."

"Far more than getting it right, is living it right," Eugene Peterson said. He goes on, "Christians don't simply learn or study or use Scripture, we assimilate it, take it into our lives in such a way that it gets metabolized into acts of love, cups of cold water, missions into all the world, healing and evangelism and justice in Jesus' name, hands raised in adoration to the Father, feet washed in the company of the Son."[9] We see the Kingdom made visible.

So how? I offer you a series of questions that may help you discover where you are to be involved.

1. What are those things that most make you come alive?
2. Who are the people that you are most burdened for?
3. If we were to each lunch together today, what would you talk about that would make your eyes light up and make you lean in to tell me more?
4. What do you see that makes you so angry you can hardly stand it?

5. What do you do that makes you so weary and spent but that just feels so worth it?

Continue to pray for God to lead you to those you are called to serve in this world.

Consider what Brad Lomenick shared at a recent Catalyst Conference: "God's calling for our life isn't a pot of gold to be found at the end of a rainbow. He wants us to simply use our gifts and passions, and He's placed them in plain sight."[10] What are the things you could easily pass over because God has placed them in plain sight?

Everyday Heroes

Among the heroes of Hurricane Harvey were the hundreds of volunteer boaters, including members of the "Cajun Navy," as they've been called, and other similar groups. These volunteers have patrolled the flooded streets of Houston in their own boats, pulling stranded families out and bringing them to safety.

"We're trying to do what we can," said Ben Theriot, an engineer whose house was flooded in last year's storms. "I had people that I barely knew showing up to help me. The best way you can thank somebody for helping you is to go help somebody else."

"You've got to try to repay the favor when someone else is in need," said one.

In Rockland, Texas, some 250 residents took shelter in an elementary school. According to ABC News, the operation was powered mostly by young people who slept in shifts and handled everything from leaks in the ceiling to making sure everyone in the building was comfortable and safe.

"At the end of the day, we're family, you know, because it brings everyone together," high school student Josh Campbell told ABC News.[11]

God wants to live through your life—you who are an everyday hero. The kingdom of God will be better for your life, stories, experiences, and skills. You can go where I cannot go. You are blessed so you can be a blessing. We are blessed so we can be a blessing (Genesis 12). The best way you can thank Someone for helping you is to go help someone else. When you give yourself for the well-being of another, your actions make the invisible Kingdom of God visible. God's Kingdom has come near.

Clare Boothe Luce was the first American woman appointed to a major ambassadorial post abroad. She said this: "There are no hopeless situations; there are only people who have grown hopeless about them."[12] We have to come to grips with this simple truth: God works through people. Not through systems, machines, computers, nations, or even organizations, words, and ideas if they are disconnected from real people. God does God's primary work through people. People like us. It changes everything when you and I put things into practice.

The first temple King Solomon built was fabulous architecturally. Exquisite gold brought glory and fame to Jerusalem, as others came to witness this achievement. However, after the exile, when the Israelites returned to rebuild the temple, everything was different. The city laid in ruins. People were sad and lacked motivation because everything they did looked insignificant. They mourned. God said, **"Do not despise the small beginnings. For the LORD rejoices to see the work begin"** (Zechariah 4:10, NLT).

Choose one thing. What one thing is the Holy Spirit leading you to put into practice? Is there one way God is leading you to serve and to lean into the problems you see in the world. Consider who you are and the gifts and passions you've been given. Your gifts aren't given in vain. God calls us to use them for the sake of others: "Therefore, my dear brothers and sisters, stand firm. Let nothing move you. Always give yourselves fully to the work of the Lord, because you know that your labor in the Lord is not in vain" (1 Corinthians 15:58). God wants to live the promises in and through our lives as a rich blessing to those around us. God wants to be incarnate in us.

> *May you know that your life and actions make visible the invisible Kingdom of God.*
>
> *May you leave learned helplessness, knowing that God desires to be incarnate in you.*
>
> *May you come alive in service, blessing those around you.*

Discussion Questions:

1. What are the biggest problems facing your community? How can you live incarnationally into those challenges?
2. Review the five questions that can help you discover where to be involved in service. Which two offer the most clarity, and what is God inviting you to do in response?
3. What is one thing the Holy Spirit is leading you to put into practice from this chapter?

―― CHAPTER SEVENTEEN ――

A Call to Bless: The Prophetic Voice

"To give someone a blessing is the most significant affirmation we can offer."

HENRI NOUWEN

WORDS HAVE TREMENDOUS POWER. Although many people have heard or said the childhood rhyme, "Sticks and stones may break our bones but words will never hurt us," we know that words *do* hurt us. Those who have suffered from verbal abuse especially know that words can be as damaging to the mind and heart as physical blows are to the body. Can you remember words that were said to you that tore you down? These words stay with us.

Words have the power to hurt and they also have the power to heal. Can you remember words that have built you up? Right now, can you think of a time when someone said something to you that made you feel known, seen, and loved? Through our words, we put one another in close proximity to God.

Beloved

I overheard a conversation with our then 3-year-old son and an adult he was meeting for the first time. "Can I call you Siah – that's short for Josiah," the adult asked. Josiah considered the question and then said thoughtfully, "No. You can call me beloved. That's what my mom calls me." I smiled with delight, happy he was getting one of the most important ways I view him: as beloved to God and to me.

We all need a reminder that we are the beloved of God. As we remind one another of our belovedness, we extend a blessing to those around us. As leaders we speak into people's lives and make space in our churches for people to remember they are beloved of God. As I live my life, my ordinary, everyday life, I want those around me to know they are beloved. In the deepest sense, I believe our calling is to remind one another of who we really are. In spite of and in the midst of the pain or challenge, you are beloved.

One of the people who does this so well is Pastor Salim Elias. Azure Hills Church has had the gift of having him here since 1976 and his consistent presence has shaped this church. As a full-time pastor, part-time pastor, and now in his retirement years as a member, Pastor Elias has spoken blessing and love into countless lives. For these last four years, I've experienced this personally. He calls us "beloved" and says, "I love you" freely and openly. He's now 96 years old and represents the tender love and nurture of God for so many of us. He offers a hand on the shoulder and a tender word, the blessing embodied in his words and the light in his eyes.

The Blessing

In Genesis 12:1-3, God tells the couple who will later become Abraham and Sarah (then Abram and Sarai), "I will bless you, so you can be a blessing." God declares, "All the peoples of the earth will be blessed through you." As we read this passage, we note that the form of this verb expresses that Abraham and Sarah will be the channel of blessing from God to all the people around them.

This is a covenant with them, yes, but unlike some of the other biblical covenantal blessings, the favor that God is extending to them doesn't stay with them alone. The way that God reveals love to them extends to those who are not in their family, and to those who don't even worship their God. Everyone who comes in contact with Abraham and Sarah will witness this love and experience this blessing! The blessing will be shared even with future generations through the success God promised to them.

In their book, *The Blessing*, Gary Smalley and John Trent talk about the importance of the blessing we have the opportunity to give to those around us, particularly those we are in a close relationship with. There are five components of a blessing that they outline, which are as follows: (1) meaningful touch, (2) a spoken message, (3) attaching high value to the one being blessed, (4) picturing a special future, and (5) an active commitment to fulfill the blessing.[1]

To bless another is to truly see them, to affirm the gift that they are, and to speak to their potential. Imagine how revolutionary it would be if every friend spoke words of blessing, if family members gave voice to what they see in one another, and if parents blessed their children each night. Imagine if church members stopped to affirm each other, sharing in gratitude the difference that the individual makes in their lives and the life of the community. Imagine if pastoral colleagues blessed each other, noticing the gifting and uniqueness in each pastor's life.

There is power in reminding one another of who we are: the beloved of God, uniquely called to a purpose here on this earth.

The Prophetic Voice

At the core of our Adventist movement is a prophetic voice that is characterized by hope. We have an optimistic outlook of both the future and the now. We hold onto this hope because Jesus has entered our hearts in the here and now and because of the promised return of our Jesus at the Second Coming. We lift our voice in hope—blessing and benefiting others we come in contact with. In people's lives we are able to see what is not yet and help them to live into that vision, because that is what we do every day. As Adventists, we wait in hope and live in a vision that is not yet. We speak hope, teach life-giving truth, and speak affirmation.

What is hope, really? **Hope is being able to see the way from where you are now to a future that is good.** It is a belief that there can be a better experience than whatever is happening in the present. It's a picture of something further than what you can see right in front of you.

Courageous hope is tenaciously calling those things that are not, as if they were. This means that in our own lives, in our church, and in the world, we believe that there is reason to expect good things. We believe this is not the end of the story for the individuals we interact with or for our church. Great things have happened. Good work is being done here. Still the prophetic voice of hope speaks to the greater days that are coming. "The best is yet to come," is the blessing we share in the midst of challenge.

If, or rather when, things feel small, futile, or hopeless for you, I pray you don't give up. **Our ministry is often in the space between—standing in the gap between what is and what will come.** It's not an easy place to be. You and I have been commissioned for the work of the gospel, the good news, that comes in this place. We are part of the redemptive movement of God in the world. It's a call to bless, not to curse. A call to affirm life wherever we find it. A call to build up others and to lean into what is not yet. To speak of things which are not as though they were (Romans 4:17).

Find Your Posse

I've been inspired by an organization called the Posse Foundation.[2] To date, nearly 10,000 students have completed college or university education while receiving full-tuition scholarships. Posse believes we must broaden the demographic representation at institutions of higher education to include students with tremendous capacity for learning who may be overlooked because of structural inequities.

Rather than traditional methods of individually awarding scholarships, Posse awards scholarships and places students in cohorts or "a posse." They meet, support, and encourage one another in this posse for all the years they are at their college or university. Due to this, and other systems of support, 90% of the students who enroll with the Posse Foundation graduate. They do it together. In the midst of challenging struggles or disadvantages, they are able to rise to be who they are called to be, even as the peers they are supporting rise alongside them. They speak hope into one another's lives.

Children of Light

In this world, it's easy to lose sight of the future and of hope. We need our lives to be shaped and framed by the hope we have in Jesus. When you and I live out the ways of God's Kingdom in our actions, words, and thoughtfulness, when we rise up to bless one another, this makes the invisible visible in the here and now. When you give yourself for the well-being of another, your actions make the invisible Kingdom of God visible, and this brings hope in what is to come.

Isaiah 9:1-2 is a prophecy. Isaiah speaks to our experience of darkness and our deepest longings. The Spirit spoke through the prophet using the symbol of Light because God knows how dark this world can be. Isaiah says to the people who were in the midst of their suffering,

"You live in darkness, but take hope, for a light is shining. I know things are dismal, but your despair will become joy. The enemy has killed people you loved and taken your land, but your oppressors will be driven away. A child will be born that will make things right...."

The darkness is real in our own lives and our world. Even though many times we get so accustomed to it that we tune out the suffering—homelessness, mental illness, cancer, divorce, heartache all around us. We, too, are "the people who sit in darkness." The darkness we see goes beyond the circle of concern for those around us; it includes the systems of injustice, suffering, and brokenness that we don't know what to do with. We sit in the darkness of fear, conflict, confusion, worry, anxiety, sadness, and hopelessness.

John 1:4 declares that Jesus is the light who comes to give us life. Jesus himself said that His disciples "will never walk in darkness, but will have the light of life" (John 8:12). In 1 Thessalonians 5:5, Paul calls the followers of God "children of light." References to light and good news are too numerous to recount here. The power of the good news is that it comes in the midst of the bad news. The power of the light is that it comes in the bleak time when we feel settled into despair. We wake up when we are blessed, affirmed, and reminded of who we are by those who come alongside us. The Kingdom that looked invisible suddenly became visible again.

Bless, Affirm, Celebrate

During the discipleship process, we make intentional time for affirmation and blessing. The words that we speak, the observations we share, and the meaningful time we take to truly see one another matters. Just as words can wound, words can heal. Words can bring out the best in us, reminding us of our belovedness. We need our "posse" who will help us to understand more of who we are.

We are not called to ignore or dismiss the reality of darkness— the pain, despair or discouragement we face. We are called rather to "repent" of it, which means "to turn" our back on it. To repent, or turn our backs on the bad news and darkness means that it no longer has the power to control our lives. Instead, we trust the power of God to bring healing and redemption, salvation and wholeness into our lives and the lives of the people around us.

We are called to bless, instead of curse. We are called to proclaim the good news in the midst of bad news. We are called to build up, instead of tear down. With our words and actions, yes, even our very lives, we bless. We face the growing fear, cynicism, death, and hopelessness and put flesh on the good news of hope, peace, and life.

We are to repent of the simple path of simply denouncing the bad. Calling attention to the darkness and letting others know you don't agree is not enough. Instead, we are to be proactive about sharing the blessing, and trust God in living the message of the Kingdom right here and now.

I Want That Kind of Blessing

Henri Nouwen was a respected professor, author, and beloved pastor. He taught at Harvard, Yale, and Notre Dame. As he was becoming dissatisfied with the life of a professor, he was called to join L'Arche Daybreak near Toronto, Canada, a community founded for people with developmental disabilities. This is where he lived until his death in 1996.

In talking about his time at L'Arche, Henri said he was suddenly with a group of people who couldn't care less about what he had taught or written or how much he knew. This experience profoundly changed his life. In various sermons and in his book, *Life of the Beloved*, Henri described this experience with one of his friends there who was "quite handicapped, but a wonderful, wonderful lady." Here is the exchange that took place between them.

> She said to me, "Henri, can you bless me?"
>
> I remember walking up to her and giving her a little cross on her forehead.
>
> She said, "Henri, it doesn't work. No, that is not what I mean."
>
> I was embarrassed and said, "I gave you a blessing."
>
> She said, "No, I want to be blessed."
>
> I kept thinking, "What does she mean?"
>
> We had a little prayer service and all these people were sitting there. After the service I said, "Janet wants a blessing." I had an alb on and a long robe with long sleeves.
>
> Janet walked up to me and said, "I want to be blessed." She put her head against my chest and I spontaneously put my arms around her, held her, and looked right into her eyes and said, "Janet, you are beautiful. We love you so much. I know you're feeling a little low right now and you need to hear again that you are beloved."
>
> She looked at me and said, "Yes, yes, yes, I know." I suddenly saw all sorts of energy coming back to her. She seemed to be relieved from the feeling of depression because suddenly she realized again that she was blessed. She went back to her place and immediately other people said, "I want a blessing, too."[3]

Yes. I want that kind of blessing. To be reminded that I am beloved. To be seen, known, and blessed is one of the greatest gifts we can offer one another.

May you remember you are the beloved of God and live daily from your belovedness.

May you find your prophetic voice of hope, as you speak into the lives of others and allow them to speak into your life as well.

May you affirm, bless, and celebrate all those you come in contact with.

Discussion Questions

1. When was a time when someone said something to you that made you feel known, seen, and loved?
2. Who is one person you can bless this week? How will you convey this blessing?
3. Take a moment to listen to the voice of God. What blessing is God speaking over you right now?

CHAPTER EIGHTEEN

Transformation: How Do We Change Anyway?

"A lifetime of transformation happens one step at a time. Move forward at the pace of grace."

GEM FADLING

IT IS A COMMON AND BEGUILING MISCONCEPTION that if people just had more information, it would automatically translate into a change in behavior. When a national or international crisis hits, if people only knew how they could help, then they would. Or in the case of social ills like racism and sexism, if only there were education about what this looks like and how others experience behavior, then people would change. The truth is, it takes more than information to bring about change. Maybe you've heard this said in your church circles as well. "If people only knew the truth, their lives would change." Thankfully, we are waking up, as a church, to the fact that **information does not equal transformation**. It is possible to know about proper nutrition and yet struggle with maintaining a nutritionally balanced diet. It is possible to know the facts about the benefits of exercise and still struggle to get moving. It is possible to have knowledge about the dynamics of healthy relationships and yet find yourself living out patterns of dysfunctional relationships. It is possible to know that Jesus loves you, and yet not live into the assurance this reality brings.

What we are discovering is that we not only need to know the truth about something, but we also need to habitually practice it in our lives, experiencing the truth over time. The same is true in our relationship with God. It is possible to know the truth about the love of God, and not experience the freedom and joy of that reality. We not only need to know the truth, but experience the Truth.

How does this happen in our lives? Ellen White shares that it is in our daily walk with Jesus that we learn and grow. "It is by communion with Him, daily, hourly—by abiding in Him—that we are to grow in grace. He is not only the Author, but the Finisher of our faith. It is Christ first and last and always. He is to be with us, not only at the beginning and the end of our course, but at every step of the way."[1]

One of our callings as a Seventh-day Adventist Church is the call to present truth. It's a calling that we can easily forget. It's a call to longing, seeking, and trusting the revelation of God in the present. In the gift of becoming established, setting our beliefs and practice as a church, we can easily forget that the journey of trust in our individual and shared life is ongoing.

Ellen White exhorts with these words:

> There is no excuse for anyone in taking the position that there is no more truth to be revealed, and that all our expositions of Scripture are without an error. The fact that certain doctrines have been held as truth for many years by our people, is not a proof that our ideas are infallible. Age will not make error into truth, and truth can afford to be fair. No true doctrine will lose anything by close investigation.[2]

Truth can handle experience, investigation, and even wrestling. The discipleship process makes space for present truth—truth that is understood and experienced in the lives of believers today, truth that moves beyond information to transformation.

How Do People Change?

This is a question particularly pertinent to understanding the effectiveness of a discipleship process. I will begin by saying that I believe the only way that lasting change takes place in our lives is through the power of the Holy Spirit. S. Joseph Kidder emphasizes the importance of the Holy Spirit's role by saying, "The greatest need of the church today is not more programs or techniques or books or seminars—it is to be filled, guided, moved, and controlled by the Holy Spirit."[3] The ultimate goal of a discipleship process is to structure space for the Holy Spirit to bring about transformation in the lives of individuals.

The discipleship process is intended to intentionally assist individuals in their formation into Christlikeness, so that the individual life is spent in ways that God desires, completely under the influence of our Loving God. This work is dependent on God and cannot be manufactured or systematized. Are there essential elements which create an environment that facilitates change? Yes. Are there things the local church can do to aid growth in the life of the believer, and make space for the Holy Spirit to work in their lives? Yes, I believe there are. Yet, it's essential to remember what part of the work is ours, and what part is God's. As with the Shekinah Glory in the Old Testament sanctuary, we create the space, but it is God who fills it (Exodus 25, 40:34-38; 2 Chronicles 7).

Structured for Change

At the foundation of the discipleship process is the desire to create uninterrupted, distraction-free space for the Holy Spirit to work in the lives of participants. Through time in the presence of God, participants experience transformation. If the local church focuses on discipleship by intentionally creating a place for people to be transformed by Jesus, live in meaningful community, and engage in purpose-giving service, individuals will develop a devotional rhythm and mission-orientation in their lives, sharing naturally as their own faith becomes more vibrant.

Discipleship Essentials

In the course of writing and implementing this discipleship process, five elements emerged as essentials to a discipleship process that leads to transformation in individuals' lives. These five are (1) a focus on Jesus, (2) the experience of the leader, (3) a healthy community, (4) a closed group setting, and (5) a long-approach to the discipleship journey. These will be expanded on below.

1. Focus of Jesus

First, in order to bring about change, the discipleship process must be centered on a relationship with Jesus, the Living Word of God, as understood through the written Word of God. As shared in previous chapters, the focal point of discipleship is Jesus. As with the original apostles, disciples of today are invited to follow Jesus and participate in His work in the world. In order for transformation to take place, the centrality of Jesus and a relationship with Him must be maintained as the focus of discipleship. The transformational process is one of a heart relationship with God, rather than a head knowledge about God.

2. The Experience of the Leader

A second essential component is the experience of the leaders who are facilitating, who set the tone for the discipleship process. The leaders must go through the process themselves, before and during the journey with others, knowing they cannot lead someone else where they have not been. Bill Hull rightly states that "the most powerful aspect of leading is modeling."[4] The leaders must be individuals who realize their own dependence on God and are willing to be models, by the grace of God, of what the life of a disciple looks like. Rather than being people with all the answers, leaders must be individuals who are appropriately vulnerable with their own relationship with God, and willing to sit with struggle, unanswered questions, and frustration on the part of participants. As the leaders become more comfortable with not answering people's questions all the time, the participants can learn to trust in God themselves. This in turn requires that leaders form an even deeper trust in God in order to point back consistently to God as the only One to be sought. The leaders set the tone for the safety of the environment, which determines to a large degree the growth that takes place within their groups.

3. Healthy Community

The third factor, the soil in which transformation grows, is a healthy community. Community must consist of relationships characterized by honesty, vulnerability, and mutual accountability. Churches can often have a great number of people in attendance on a weekend, yet offer little depth of relationships, namely because there is no time or place for substantial relationships to form. Still, what people are hungering for most is community. A discipleship process, whether in Sabbath School or another midweek group, allows people space to experience transformation in their lives. The Holy Spirit works through the community to root them. As participants learn to be honest, vulnerable, and accountable to one another, they are able to carry those qualities into their relationship with God.

4. Closed Group Setting

A fourth, and related, characteristic that assists in building transformational relationships is that the discipleship group is a closed group—a group whose members remain consistent throughout the entire 12-week journey. Group members make up a covenant with one another to be present each week and hold each other accountable to be there. One participant mentioned that the time spent with the same group of people allowed for the group to go deep, beyond the superficial. This intimacy in the group occurs when trust forms through sustained experience with one another. Both the leader and participants make the 12-week commitment to show up and be present to the work God is doing in their midst.

5. A Long Approach to Discipleship

The final feature of discipleship groups that influence change is that they instill in participants a long approach to the spiritual journey. Wendy Walshe points out, "You cannot sit in the presence of God without being changed. You may feel like nothing is happening, but it is—even if imperceptible to you at the time."[5] A discipleship process is not a certificate to be earned or something to be checked off a spiritual "to do" list, but is instead an ongoing, journey-oriented approach to life. The participants are invited to walk with Jesus and join Him in His work, trusting that "He who started the work will carry it to completion" (Philippians 1:6). This process-oriented approach encourages patience in the participants towards themselves and others. It revitalizes the need to continue on in prayer, Bible study, and service, even if the participants cannot discern the difference it is making in their life. Change takes time and patience.

In conclusion, the elements necessary for change and transformation through a discipleship process are a focus on Jesus Christ as the center of the process; a leader who has experienced what they are seeking to facilitate; healthy community characterized by honesty, vulnerability, and mutual accountability; a closed group, and finally, patience with the change process itself.

Results

As participants reflected on their experience in the group, one factor that emerged as one of the primary catalysts for growth was community. The way the group members interacted and shared life together was a powerful experience. Participants expressed feeling less isolated on Sabbath mornings when the church gathers, because they now knew people more closely, and were likewise known by others. Members were now more than smiling faces wishing them a "Happy Sabbath," and were instead people with back stories and depth.

Participants expressed the fact that the discipleship process helped them to deepen their intimacy and trust with other believers; to experience a greater frequency in their praise and prayer life; to renew their devotion to God; to slow down and spend time with God in His Word; to change their perspective on facing trials and struggle; and to step outside their comfort zone to serve and bless others. They got a taste of the sweetness of God's Presence. God used this process to strengthen their devotion to Jesus and relationship with Him.

Throughout the focus-group interview, discipleship participants expressed a change in their commitment to and participation in the mission of Christ. One of the most profound changes was in the life of one male participant who recounted the following:

> Before I started this discipleship process, I didn't pray in public. I guess I was looking at myself. I promised God that I'm going to start praying in church. I've got to let God take complete control of my life and quit thinking that I've got to prove something to others—instead I'll just be myself and He'll do the rest.

This participant entered into a new-found freedom that he affirms has persisted to this day, years later. Certainly, discovering their spiritual gifts and affirming one another in those gifts was a highlight of the discipleship process. However, it did not stop with simply identifying their gifts. Many in the group went on to try new ministries where they could put those gifts into practice, including ministry coordinating, prayer ministry, media ministry, leading a class on how to give a Bible study, and hospitality ministry—applying missional living to their own lives and context.

Transformation in participants' lives was the most profound part of this journey. Two discipleship class participants recounted that they were able to see the growth God had done in their lives through an encounter they had had a month after the discipleship class concluded. There was an evangelistic event at the church. The group was gathered together, and the person who was going to pray with the church volunteers, as well as welcome and pray with the community guests to start the program, was not there. Formerly, both individuals were afraid to pray with others, especially in public. Describing this incident, they said they looked at one another and said three simple words, "Remember discipleship class." Instead of leaving to find someone else, one of them prayed with the volunteers before the event and the other welcomed and prayed with the gathered community guests. This was a radical change in their lives! Their closeness to God and each other meant they were more willing to be available to God at that moment.

As Bill Hull summarizes, "Evangelism will result from proper discipleship. The lack of passion for the Great Commission comes from a lack of character – a lack of spiritual depth – rather than a lack of strategic vehicles for reaching others."[6] It is my conviction that as the church focuses on discipling members in the character of Christ, spiritual depth will increase, and a passion for witness and service will result.

Remember Who Does the Work

One Sabbath, after our weekly fellowship meal at Azure Hills Church, John, one of our amazing deacons, was moving tables back into the storage closet. Little Samuel was around 3 years old at the time and wanted to help. John invited him to hold one end of the table, while John carried the other end. John and Samuel walked several tables to the storage closet that way, John lifting the table on one end and Samuel resting his little hand on the other end of the table, walking with him.

This is the picture of our work with God in the discipleship process. God delights in our partnership, but let's make sure we remember who is doing the "heavy lifting." The change in our own lives and in the lives of those we serve, comes from God. We create the space, we are invited into the process, but God brings the transformation.

May you surrender to the good news that all transformation comes from God – in your life or in the lives of others.

May you relentlessly focus on creating uninterrupted, distraction-free space for the Holy Spirit to work, for God's glory to be experienced.

May you walk in freedom and humility, realizing it is God who does the heavy lifting.

Discussion Questions

1. Which of the five elements essential to the discipleship process does your church excel at? Which one is in need of the most growth?
2. Which of the discipleship process results stories was most inspiring to you?
3. What is one area in your life, or the life of your church, where you can receive the gift of trusting that it is God who does the heavy lifting?

CHAPTER NINETEEN

Process, Not Destination

"Faith isn't about having everything figured out ahead of time; faith is about following the quiet voice of God without having everything figured out ahead of time."

RACHEL HELD EVANS

AS STATED EARLY ON, I believe there is nothing more important than prioritizing (1) being a disciple and (2) joining God in making disciples. Yet, on the journey towards that goal, there are unexpected stops—things that waylay us and circumstances that don't cooperate with our plans.

To each of us who are struggling—with health issues, with difficult relationships, with budgets that just won't balance, with hard days, with distractions—remember this promise: "Being confident of this, that he who began a good work in you will carry it on to completion until the day of Christ Jesus" (Philippians 1:6).

By the phrase, "until the day of Christ Jesus," we understand that apparently God is clear on something we often forget: change takes time. Patience means "to accept or tolerate delay." Maybe that's why it's listed among the fruits of the Spirit in Galatians 5. It doesn't come naturally to us, but is something **supernatural** that happens when God comes and lives in us.

Being a Christ-follower means seeing redemption in every situation, in every person, in every relationship, in every church, realizing that all the way up to "the day of Christ Jesus," God is working change in us and in everyone around us. In order to be a force for good for the Kingdom of God in the world, we must persist even when the natural temptation is to give up. We must press on, despite delay—in hope, in belief that God is at work, *even* in the situation you're facing now. Change takes time. I'm praying for you and I, even now, that we may have the grace, the hope, and the patience to press on.

In the process of writing and implementing this discipleship curriculum, I realized my own addiction to seeing change in a short amount of time. The perfect example of this is the first discipleship class I had. I prepared many pages of teaching notes and a long list of content to cover. As the session progressed, I discovered that I was approaching the discipleship process as if all that the participants needed in order to experience change was the right information; *then* they would have a stronger relationship with Jesus! I was acting as if information about a relationship with Jesus would develop a relationship with Jesus in the participants. What God started to make clear 30 minutes into the first journey group, and affirmed in subsequent groups, was that transformation in the life of God's people takes place experientially, in a relationship with God and with other believers, and this takes time. There are no short-cuts to the discipleship process. There is no quick and easy program to implement. Through experiencing a relationship with Christ and His followers, disciples are born.

Changed by the Process

God has brought about dramatic change in my own life and ministry through this process, and continues to bring change in me through this journey. I don't have it all figured out. In fact, I am now asking new questions while exploring what it means to focus on discipleship in the local church, and especially what my role as pastor is in this process. Still, even with more to learn, I can see that I have grown in heart and mind. I have seen changes in the following areas.

Delight in God

I enjoy time in prayer and in the Word as one relating to a dear friend. I have loved God since the day I accepted Jesus as my Savior. Through this journey, however, I learned new ways of relating to God that have made my experience even richer. I love God and am even more rooted now in God's love for me. One key is that I have a deeper understanding that God does not love me because of what I do or how I perform. God simply loves me, and I am free to love in response. It is a privilege to bring this personal experience into the process of discipleship with others.

Goals in Ministry

I have found that my relationship with God has rooted me so I am able to move forward in taking risks for God's Kingdom, experiencing success and failure knowing that it is not about me, but about the greater purpose of God. My goals now center around nurturing leaders and systems that disciple others. Discipleship can happen in any area of ministry—in the media ministry or on a capital campaign. The question is, How are we being and growing disciples of Jesus in this process? Where is God working among us?

This discipleship journey has shaped the way that I approach my goals and direction in ministry.

Focus on Discipleship

As a pastor, implementing this discipleship journey each time has provided a way to focus on discipling and growing people in Christ. Through this process, I have become convinced that everything else I do will most likely be forgotten—programs, sermons, and board meetings. Yet, those individuals for whom I have been a part of teaching how to connect with God will continue to bear fruit in their lives in the years to come. These ones who have discovered how to pray, listen, and read the Word, who have discovered their spiritual gifts and put them into practice, who have moved from isolation to connection with the body of believers—for these ones, discipleship has made a difference. There are so many things pulling for my attention as a pastor. Discipling others and teaching them to disciple is an essential part of what God invites me to do with my time. This process has brought focus, passion, and life to my heart and ministry.

Blessed by Community

More than ever before, this process revealed the importance of shared journey. God has led me to experientially learn vulnerability and trust through the Presence of God with others. I had no idea, when I started this journey ten years ago, of the painful, personal suffering I would experience. This taught me that we are not meant to do life alone—even, and perhaps especially as leaders, elders, and pastors. This year marks nine years of guarding annual spiritual retreat time with three colleagues in ministry. The sacred space of time together in God's presence has changed me. Through it all, God has been faithful and constant in Presence. As leaders, I have realized that God desires us to experience community, not only facilitate it for others. It has been a profound and sacred experience to be used in other people's lives and to see how God uses them to bless my life. Through this personal experience in community, it has become clear to me that it is absolutely essential that discipleship be facilitated in the context of community. Community is how we grow, learn, and heal. Through the difficult blessing of vulnerability and pain, I can recognize some ways to lead others where God is taking me.

New Understanding

There are many reasons for the inner strength that I possess. Chalk it up to a combination of God-given personality, emerging from a lineage of strong people, and going through tough situations. Certainly, serving as a pastor in a denomination which does not yet fully recognize and affirm women in this role develops inner strength. God has been teaching me dependence, how to lean into strength that is not my own. This is indeed a great paradox, for strength and weakness are both gifts in God's hand. The role of the disciple is to surrender self to God and let God decide what is needed for the glory of the Kingdom. I now define strength as vulnerable surrender to God and to others. Strength is willingness to give myself with abandon to God, for God's purpose. Whether that looks like faith in the midst of brokenness or faith in rejoicing is up to God to decide.

No Shortcuts

Through this journey, I discovered my own desire for a shortcut. As a pastor I was still searching for a "magic bullet" that would rapidly change members into Christlikeness and grow the church numerically. I wanted transformation in a rush. God's invitation was for me to abide and let God do the work. There is no shortcut to growth. Change takes time. What matters most is making time in community for people to encounter the Living God, which results in transformation. This is something only the Holy Spirit can work in our lives. I, as pastor, can facilitate transformation by creating opportunities where people can experience God; however, there is no shortcut to the slow change that comes by consistently being in God's presence. I have discovered peace in God's promise to finish the work that has been started in each person (Philippians 1:6).

The outcome of this journey has been and continues to be more lasting, deep, and life-altering than I expected. I set out to create an experiential discipleship process for the local church, facilitated in community that inspires an increase in devotional life and mission involvement. By God's grace, I've witnessed ongoing change in my own life and the lives of those around me. I am deeply grateful for what God is doing in my life, heart, and leadership through this ongoing journey. I desire this change to permeate all aspects of my ministry as I continue growing and leading from a place of dependence on Jesus Christ.

Dead or Dormant

A church member and friend described that when they first moved into their place, the landscaping had been sitting in the California sun for months without any attention. They called the local nursery to come help them with new landscaping. The owner is a master gardener, having spent decades planting and nurturing growing things of all types. Our friends thought the entire area needed to be ripped up and that they would have to start over.

Patiently, the owner went around to all the plants and said to begin watering. He pointed out several that were dead and needed to be removed, but said to water the others. "These are dormant and they will come back to life when they are watered."

Friends, we cannot tell the difference between what is dormant and what is dead. We don't know what will spring back to health with the water of life or what needs to be removed so that there is space for a new planting. This is true in the soil of our own lives, as well as in the lives of those around us.

As we are willing to recognize that discipleship is about process, not destination, about the ongoing nurture of our soul's garden, I believe God will settle us into a new experience in our ministry—an abiding, discipleship-focused outlook that will change every part of what we do. Sermons on Sabbath morning, board meetings, worship talks with Adventurers and Pathfinders, and one-on-one conversations all take on a different focus in light of the slow work of God in the discipleship process that is taking place in each person, including ourselves.

Trust the Process

"Mama, Mama, Mama!!!"

I'm at the kitchen sink. My daughter is at the dining room table about 10 feet away and within sight of me.

"Mama!! Hug!" she cries out.

Insistent. Loud. Unrelenting.

I go over and enfold her in my embrace. She lays her head sideways on my shoulder and her arms wrap around my neck. I close my eyes, suddenly caught up in the moment. I want to remember this feeling forever.

"There were many years where you wanted exactly this," my husband Caleb says as he watches us.

It's true. I wanted this. The very thing I'm experiencing right in this moment is something I longed for for a very long time. That's how it is, isn't it? Full of longing and desire and then, a transition to the experience, the fulfillment. Perhaps it's the sleep loss and the craziness that is parenting young children, but I must admit, I do have moments I forget. When I am in it all the time, I am unable to be continuously aware that I am living with my desire fulfilled.

It's not that this is always the case. Many times, I sit with the longing and the desire that doesn't go away and doesn't get to be fulfilled, at least in the way I hoped. Those are painful. But with those things that do come, with the gifts that enter my life after prayer and tears, I want to pay attention. I want to notice on a regular basis. So, I am committed to pausing regularly to simply settle into the reality that I am now living and experiencing the very gift I once desired.

This is also true of the growth you've experienced in your own life. This is true for how discipleship growth takes place in our churches. The thing which we pray for and desire is often the thing we hardly notice once we have it. Let's pause to settle into this gift, to notice what God is doing in your life and in your church or organization or department. Commit to pausing to notice the process God is working in you and those around you. For truly, it is a beautiful thing.

"Those who sow with tears will reap with songs of joy.
Those who go out weeping,
carrying seed to sow, will return with songs of joy,
carrying sheaves with them"

(Psalm 126:5-6).

On the other side of tears is joy. On the other side of your prayers for growth in your life and in your church is fulfillment. On the other side of seeds planted in the earth are sheaves carried in your arms. The only way is through all of those experiences. Through the tears, the prayers, the planting and the harvest, God invites you to trust the work of God in you. God is working in this process of discipleship in you, in your family, in your church, and in all those you serve. Trust God's process.

May you show up and surrender to the good work God is doing in you.

May you recognize the places God is fulfilling your prayers and your longings.

May you know deeply that you can trust the process of what God is doing in you, and the promise of God to complete the good work God has started.

Discussion Questions

1. Are there any areas of your life where you're trusting more in right information than right relationship with God? How might God be inviting you into an experiential process instead?
2. As a church leader, what are three of the things that call for most of your time? What can you do to give discipleship a higher priority on your list?
3. What is one aspect of your life in which God is inviting you to trust the process? What is something you can express gratitude for how God has fulfilled your desires?

CHAPTER TWENTY

Where Do You Go From Here?

"So then, just as you received Christ Jesus as Lord, continue to live in Jesus, rooted and built up in him, strengthened in the faith as you were taught, and overflowing with thankfulness."

COLOSSIANS 2:6–7

ALL THROUGHOUT THE SCRIPTURES, the word 'Behold' is used. This word can be translated from the original languages as, "Look" or "Pay Attention" or "See!" It's a marker of emphasis, calling people to focus or center one's mind on what's about to happen next.

- In Genesis, God gives every herb and plant of the beautiful, perfect world to the man and woman at the beginning of the creation and says, "Behold."
- In Exodus, God says to Moses, "Behold" the cry of the Israelites, my people who are in slavery. Look... pay attention... see their suffering.

- In Isaiah 43, God says, "Behold" the new thing I am doing among you. In the wilderness a straight path is being marked out. Pay attention to this work I am doing.

- In Matthew 1, God says, "Behold" a virgin will conceive and you will call His name Emmanuel, God with us. He will forgive His people from their sins.

As you go through this process of implementing a discipleship journey or experience, I want to encourage you to behold. *Look. See. Pay Attention.* To what God is doing in your midst, to the good gifts God has brought, to the way your cries are answered, to the way God makes for you where there was no way. To the transformation in your life and in the lives of those around you.

"If I were to begin life again," Jules Renard said, "I should want it as it was. I would only open my eyes a little more."[1]

I encourage you to take notes, physically recording the miracles, events, and happenings you see, and how God works in you. It doesn't have to be anything fancy – just a text document on your computer or a simple notebook where you write the ways God is working. By this time next year, you can look back and read all the many ways you beheld the Almighty God at work.

I encourage you and I to pause and behold.

"When the LORD saw that he had gone over to look, God called to him from within the bush, 'Moses! Moses!'

And Moses said, 'Here I am.'

'Do not come any closer,' God said. 'Take off your sandals, for the place where you are standing is holy ground'" (Exodus 3:4-5).

Pause for a moment. Take off your shoes and recognize the holy God working in the midst of your ordinary life and ministry.

What Matters Most

When asked which commandment was the greatest, Jesus replied, "Love the Lord your God with all your heart. . . [and] Love your neighbor as yourself" (Mark 12:30, 31). It is these two inseparable demonstrations of love that this discipleship curriculum seeks to uphold and teach in an experiential way. The love of God seen in the devotional life, and the love of neighbor, as manifested in community and acts of witness and service to others. There are many questions left unanswered. There is constant trial and error as we seek to follow the Holy Spirit in our context with the people God has given us to serve alongside. Still, after the past 10 years leading this particular discipleship journey, I can say that intentionally implementing an experiential discipleship process curriculum does make space for God to grow disciples. As a pastor, this journey has made a difference in my own practice as a disciple myself and the way that I am a part of nurturing growth in the disciples around me. Inviting people into an experience increases growth in relationship with God, community, and purpose (witness and service).

Though good content is essential to the discipleship process, a discipleship curriculum does not have to be fancy or complicated in order to bring about change. In fact, the opposite is true: simplicity in applying the biblical principles of discipleship increases accessibility, making the process more approachable for participants. The invitation of God through the Scriptures is to form habits of seeking God in prayer, reading God's Word, worship, witnessing, service, and confession, among other practices, all in the context of the community of Christ.

The Great Commission (Matthew 28:18-20) highlights the importance of developing the practice of being with God, obeying God's voice, and teaching others to do the same. By its very nature, discipling is something that is modeled and lived out in relationship as the primary way of teaching (1 Corinthians 11; Philippians 3:17).

Perhaps it isn't surprising that even the simplicity of the command to make disciples is often overlooked by the church. Instead, programs, events, and committees demand our attention. Even information-packed discipleship Bible studies can become substitutes for relational, experiential disciple-making. I get it. I'm in the trenches of ministry and feel this pressure too. The church is in danger of missing the Great Commission (Matthew 28:18-20) in favor of trying to keep all the plates of ministry spinning or to stay on the path of church growth through a busy evangelism schedule. The biblical witness and my own experience with this process attest to this truth: lasting growth comes from the transforming power of God through the Holy Spirit, realized in the community of believers, over time. The goal of the church, and more specifically local church leadership, is to create a space where people can come in contact with God. This happens in discipleship groups, Sabbath School classes, Adventurer and Pathfinder groups, and other places where we gather. The question is, will we be intentional about what we are doing in the way we grow disciples? If discipleship is the first priority, it will shape the way we engage the rest of our ministry.

Engaging Leaders

In this important work of being and growing disciples, and particularly in grounding our work as leaders and pastors in discipleship, it's important to find partners on the journey. One of the many possible ways to develop synergy between yourself and other leaders in your church or ministry context is to engage in a discipleship journey together. As you actively experience the presence of God together through the journey, the natural response is to desire for others to have the same experience. Over the years, as elders and other key leaders have participated with me, it has opened up deeper avenues for prayer and greater synergy of ministry between myself and them.

Bill Hull recommends creating a prototype discipleship group made up exclusively of leaders.[2] This group meets together for a set period of time, which is determined based on the length of time the groups will meet, if and when these leaders facilitate. If a 12-week group length will be used, like this curriculum, then the leader's group will meet for 12-weeks. This is a great way to inspire a new experience with God among elders, Sabbath School teachers, or small group leaders.

Following the discipleship journey with the leaders, they could each be empowered to lead their own discipleship group of 8-12 individuals or use their new experience in their area of ministry (i.e., their Sabbath School class). The pastor would then continue to meet with the leaders' group, even as they moved forward with facilitating their own groups. This is a healthy model that continues to provide support to the leaders, while spreading the reach and influence of the discipleship process.[3]

This book, *Deep Calling: on being and growing disciples,* can be a helpful additional resource for leaders, elders, or pastors to go through together, reflecting on the discussion questions at the end of each chapter, sharing what they agree or disagree with, and how this best applies in their context. The goal of the *Deep Calling Curriculum* is to make the discipleship process structured and simple for the leader to engage and lead others through the process. This is a curriculum that the pastor, leader, or elder can use to take others through the process in groups as small as four or as large as 16.

What is Required to Move a Church Toward a Focus on Discipleship?

First, it is imperative that a shift toward discipleship in the local church be unashamedly centered on Jesus Christ, experientially discipling members in both how to pursue an intimate relationship and how to join Jesus in mission and service, both in the context of community.

Second, discipleship requires a focus on people. Discipleship is not another program of the church, something members can check off on their spiritual "to do" list. Instead, it is the essential process of transformation into Christlikeness that takes place in relationship with God and other believers.

Finally, the pastor and church leaders must be willing to think small in order to see big change. Experiencing God in a discipleship process with other believers holds powerful, world-shifting moments for participants. Change does happen, and this change is a catalyst for Christ-centered living. However, this change takes time. Leaders must be willing to take a micro approach as opposed to a macro approach to change and church growth. Think first about the individual. As one small group experiences change, the ripple effect moves on to affect the entire congregation.

The goal is to form disciples who make disciples, who, in turn, make more disciples—spreading the passion, love, and service of Christ. George Barna appeals, "When we get our priorities right, everything falls into line. True discipleship must be a priority within the church. In fact, without a heavy emphasis upon discipleship, there is no church . . . never, never stop molding people into Christlikeness."[4] As Jesus said, "A disciple is not above his teacher, but everyone when he is fully trained will be like his teacher" (Luke 6:40). The desire of Jesus was that His followers would become like Him, their teacher. Then, in turn, others would join the ranks as Jesus' disciples, believing in God through their message (John 17:20), discipled in the way of Jesus by other disciples who are following God in their own lives.

While there is much more that we can learn about implementing a discipleship journey in the church, this curriculum is a place for you to begin and develop. Use and adapt it in your context, as the Holy Spirit leads you. We keep in mind the goal that through the experiential discipleship process, members become more like Christ, learning how to love God with all their heart and their neighbors as themselves (Mark 12:30-31). As they follow Jesus, they learn to disciple others in the same way (Matthew 28:18-20). **This will change the world, one person at a time.** We may not see this change during our time at the places we serve. There will be growth going on that we won't catch a glimpse of. In the words of the 19th century poet Henry Newbolt, we are called to "build for the days we shall not see."[5] As we disciple others, we are building and investing in people for the years to come.

Who Will We Become?

Many people, including myself, start off the New Year with goals. I prayerfully ask God what I need to focus on for growth during the year and invite God to lead me to end the year in a different place than I started. As I recently read James Clear's best-selling book, *Atomic Habits*, I was struck with his reframe of the New Year. Instead of trying to create resolutions this year, he invited readers to ask, "What kind of person am I becoming?"[6] In other words, get clear on the kind of person that you want to be, and then live towards that picture.

As believers, this is similar to the focus we have as we trust the work God is doing in our lives. There is a vision of the person we are becoming that each of us can move towards by the grace of God. A person strengthened in our inner being by the Spirit, with Christ dwelling in our hearts through love. A person rooted and established in love. A person filled with the fullness of God and experiencing above and beyond what we could ask or imagine because of the riches of Jesus (Ephesians 3:16-21).

Genesis 1:1 says, "In the beginning God created the heavens and the earth…" Then at the end, or rather the beginning, God says,

"Behold, I am making all things new..." (Revelation 21:5). History is moving towards a glorious end and a new beginning! God is at work in our lives for the sake of our transformation, a transformational work that will only be complete at the Second Coming of Jesus. Hold onto courage and hope for the work God is doing, both in your life and in the life of the church.

Deep Roots

One of my dad's dreams was to visit China. When he was diagnosed with stage 4 cancer in 2005, I encouraged him to seize the moment and visit the place so many of his friends had talked about. We set out together – my dad, my brother Tyler, my husband Caleb, and I. We toured China for 25 days. We traveled from the northern cities of Beijing and Dalian, then to the south by train to Xian and Shanghai. It was an unforgettable trip. We explored, soaked in the history, and made lasting memories.

During our travels we visited many temples and gardens. In one garden, we wandered over the bridges and through each gate, seeing breathtaking vegetation. In front of an outcrop of towering bamboo, this is what was shared with us: There are varieties of bamboo that, when planted, show no signs of growth for up to four years. Then, in the fifth year, the plant can grow up to 40 feet in that one year! When it looks like nothing is happening, roots are growing invisibly beneath the surface, giving the plant the support to sustain the growth that is coming.

You cannot sit alone in the presence of God, with the Word, inviting the Holy Spirit, and have nothing happen. You may not be aware of something happening, but it is happening. When you're sitting there and you think nothing is happening, roots are deepening to sustain the growth that is coming in your life.

Likewise, leaders, you cannot make space for discipleship in your church, inviting people to experience the presence of God, the Word, and the transforming power of the Holy Spirit, and have nothing happen. You may not be aware of all that's happening, but it is happening. Roots are sinking in deep to sustain the growth that is coming for the individuals participating, as well as for the church.

You cannot be in the presence of God without being changed.

May you realize today that you are standing on holy ground; stand barefoot and in awe.

May you take a closer look at God working in your midst, make space, and celebrate the work God is doing.

May you grow in patience, as God is growing deep roots in you to sustain the growth and fruitfulness coming in your life and ministry.

Discussion Questions

1. Where in your life is God inviting you to pause and behold?
2. Who could be in your prototype discipleship group of leaders?
3. What is the one next step that God is calling you to take as a result of our time together in this book?

CHAPTER TWENTY-ONE

And Then, Everything Changed...

IT'S AN OVERSTATEMENT to say everything changed. Certainly our God, the Scriptures, and our identity in Christ did not change, praise God. However, the way we lived and worked, participated in church life and served our community has dramatically changed. At the time of this writing we still sit with uncertainty due to a virus that has, at best, upended our plans and, at worst, caused deep loss of life and financial stability.

Originally, this book was going to be released at the North American Division CALLED convention in June 2020. Instead, we found ourselves adjusting plans and adding to our daily vocabulary words like pandemic, quarantine, and shelter-at-home. We changed our patterns to minimize time outside, not to mention the daily use of face masks and hand sanitizer wherever we went.

Life has changed. Depending on where you call home, this season has perhaps looked different for you. We aren't able to meet and worship, study and pray, love and serve as a church in the same ways as we could before. Yet, the need to be and grow disciples is more needed now than before.

I add this chapter, not because I have this figured out. I'm finding my footing in this new environment just as you are. Still, right now, at this time, I want to give voice and space for the ongoing need to explore creative options for discipleship.

Pastoral care and leadership during this pandemic have looked very different. Holding space for weeping and grief on the phone or over FaceTime, instead of being able to show up in person. Leaving gifts on the doorstep for elderly members (quarterlies, flowers, or books), waving and "air hugging" from outside their window. Rallying people to participate in a "love flood" of messages for someone or a "card campaign" to share care to those quarantining at home. Celebrating milestone birthdays with "drive by" parades, leaving cards and blowing kisses while maintaining distance. Delivering comfort food to essential workers or those who feel like they just can't do another day of heartbreak. I've witnessed the meaningful impact of virtual anointing services, video messages gathered and edited for grieving families, and meal trains with restaurant takeout.

The church continues to be the body of Christ, my friends. Being and growing disciples is about adapting to what love in action looks like, even and perhaps especially when the landscape changes. What does it look like to live in peace now? What does it look like to take to heart God's promise to, "Be still and know that I am God" (Psalm 46:10)? What does it look like to "be the hands and feet of Jesus" when we aren't interacting in the same ways we were before? For many, this season has been one of heightened anxiety, stress, and fear. The *Deep Calling* discipleship process gives space for bringing those feelings and stressors into the presence of the One who is able to heal and strengthen and bring hope. This is not dependent on the ability to meet together in person. Discipleship through an intentional process is possible through an in-person experience, virtual experience, or a hybrid delivery.

Hybrid Delivery

It's hard to believe it took me this long to say the word Zoom in this chapter. Zoom has become such an integral part of our lives. We've used this platform to host church board, finance committee, elders' meetings, prayer meetings, and weekly Sabbath Schools. While some churches have been broadcasting sermons each week on YouTube, others have gathered as a church over (you guessed it!) Zoom. Video conferencing has changed our ability to meet together and it is an exceptional tool for facilitating a discipleship process.

There are many options for online video conferencing. Zoom is the one I have used the most, yet others have become outspoken in their appreciation for Google Hangouts/Google Meet and Skype Meet Now. All of these platforms have the capability to connect participants from their own homes via video conferencing. If you haven't yet needed to use video conferencing, watch a tutorial video about the features of each of these applications and see which one you prefer.

The *Deep Calling Curriculum* can be implemented in person or virtually, or a combination of the two. For this fall, I am currently planning on some sessions in person outside and some online, with the ability to move to exclusively online should the need arise.

This book, as well as the companion *Deep Calling Curriculum*, model engagement in a discipleship process for the local church. The same principles that apply when meeting in person apply in the online context. The model of pairs, groups of four, and then larger group processing can be done in the online world by enabling breakout rooms in Zoom. You are able to do this during the meeting or, even better, you can pre-assign participants to breakout rooms. After the first meeting you will know who is in a small group together and pre-assigning makes breaking people into those groups very easy during a meeting. The facilitator is able to join any breakout room, just as you would walk around the room among the small groups, pausing to listen in or lend support.

The advantage of starting off in person is that people have a reference point for one another. I recommend that if you are able to do one retreat or the opening meeting outside, with masks, and giving plenty of space to participants, (following whatever the current recommended safety guidelines are), it will be well worth it, as the connection will have begun person-to-person as the Holy Spirit moves among you.

As the leader or facilitator, you may want to consider teaching with distance between you and the participants for added safety if you are not wearing a mask, or check out "smile masks" that offer a clear area for your mouth so that those who rely on lip reading will be better able to understand you. Additionally, "smile masks" allow participants the opportunity to see your facial expressions and are better for communication.

Service

Many of the service opportunities you would have previously offered may no longer be available to you. Brainstorm some new options in your area, using some of the following ideas to get your creative thoughts going.

Pack Pantry Boxes

Due to job loss and financial struggle, there are many who can use extra support right now. Provide a list of non-perishables that nearly every family can use. Invite discipleship participants to buy pantry staples (as they are able to). Now pack these into pantry boxes (perhaps including a grocery store gift card from the church to buy fresh veggies and fruits). Make sure you ask people to discreetly share what they can bring by emailing or texting you so that you can purchase extra items in case participants are not able to afford this expense. Include hand-written cards expressing hope and prayers for the recipients.

Treat the Staff
Consider taking lunch to the staff that work in a Senior Center or hospital close to your church. Have discipleship participants donate money towards takeout or buy various parts of the menu to assemble in a meal. Write out cards of gratitude and affirmation. Then go together to drop it off. Hold brightly painted signs of appreciation so that each participant is involved. "Surprise! You're loved and appreciated!"

Donate Blood
Many blood banks and hospitals have been struggling to keep up with demand through this crisis. Show up en force to donate blood. What better thing to offer than to give the gift of life. Be sensitive to the fact that some do not qualify to donate blood, or for some other reason are unable to. You will want to have more than one option.

Cards, Flowers, Fruit
These are the days of intense isolation and loneliness. Write out meaningful cards and gather flowers or fruit to leave on the doorsteps of seniors or those spending time in quarantine. Maybe it's someone's birthday or maybe they just lost a job. You may create a list of members in the church and community who can use extra love, then invite discipleship participants to take to the streets.

Support Small Business Owners
Small businesses are struggling. It has been a difficult season, full of uncertainty and instability. Invite discipleship participants to take the time to pray with small business owners in the area around your church and leave them a reminder of your presence. For example: pack a gift bag with a mug with your church logo and website on it with tea and hot chocolate. Add a card that says you value their

business and you are praying for them during this difficult time. Divide the names of businesses among the spiritual companion pairs and invite them to go to the businesses and pray.

Alternative Ways to Connect

As a leader you want to provide participants with the chance to go deeper. Previously this looked like gathering them for food and games at your house or in the church fellowship hall. For many areas of the country, this is not an option or not advised at this time. This should not hold us back from providing ways for people to connect. Here are a few ideas.

Blanket Island Social

Invite participants to bring their blanket and picnic dinner to the church lawn for a night of fun. This time, instead of mingling like old times, everyone is invited to stay on their "blanket island" (social distancing made easy). Mark out blanket spots ahead of time, let people choose their landing spot, and let the games begin! Games like *Would You Rather* or a remix of *The Newlywed Game* lend themselves well to this distanced-remix.[1] This provides a good way for participants to share about themselves, without sharing germs.

Tailgate Social

Invite participants to bring their own drink and snack to a tailgate social. Mark spaces ahead of time in the church parking lot to create a "circle" with vehicles. Everyone needs to stay at the back of their own vehicle (either sitting on the tailgate or their trunk) and socialize. As the facilitator, you will ask people questions and offer prizes for the questions you invite them to participate in. Consider a prize for the best decorated vehicle or tie balloons and streamers to the vehicles as they enter the parking lot.

Game Night Over Zoom

Grab your favorite snack and join me in your living room… and mine. Well, let's all just stay in our own living rooms this time. With video conferencing, we can still take some time to laugh and get to know each other. Many games lend themselves to Zoom gatherings. For example, 2 *Truths and a Lie* is a game that will have people guessing new facts about each other, getting to know one another in new ways. You can use Kahoot! (https://kahoot.com) to create a quiz using information from participants gathered ahead of time. The options are endless as you use this platform for Saturday night fun.

Cooking Over Zoom

Choose a gifted chef from your congregation or pay a local restaurant owner to lead the group in making a delicious recipe they'll love. Give out your ingredient list ahead of time, instruct each participant to gather the supplies, and get ready to bond! Whether you opt for a dessert, snack, or main course, it's sure to bring people together. For example, making spring rolls brought one small group closer to each other and gave them a tasty treat in the process.[2]

Tools

In the discipleship process detailed here in this book, you've seen ways to interact, connect, and serve that need to be adjusted for the times we are facing now. One of the challenges is to modify the delivery, but keep the meaning. For example, in Sessions 7 and 8 entitled "Finding Your Purpose, Part 1 and 2," there is a powerful exercise for creating a "Spiritual Gifts Poster." Participants write their discoveries of who they are and receive affirmation from other participants. One way to do this virtually is by using Padlet (https://padlet.com/). Each participant can create a free poster board online, sharing more of who they are, how they are gifted, and who they are passionate about serving. This content is only accessible to those who have the link. These links can be emailed to the discipleship group and participants can read and comment in affirmation (just as they would write those affirmations on the posters hung around the room). Additionally, the facilitator/leader of the discipleship group can use Padlet to share content with participants or to create a shared "Praise and Prayer Wall" where participants can celebrate or intercede for each other.

Tools like Google Docs and Google Drive can be helpful for sharing information with participants. Just like Zoom and Kahoot! mentioned earlier, Padlet and Google Docs provide ways for groups to interact in an online environment. You may have your favorite online tools or social media sites. Imagine how you can use those tools in new ways to deliver information, create shared experience and connection, and inspire service in a discipleship process.

We Need You Now

For some people, this crisis has drawn them in nearer to their Savior. Others have found their connection with God strained. Perhaps they have had little time to spend or have found themselves coping with feelings of overwhelm in unhealthy ways. Now is the time to invite growth through an intentional discipleship process. People are wondering what it means to use their gifts at a time like this. They may find themselves with questions about what God wants from them in crisis. Now is the time to create space for the much-needed movement of the Holy Spirit among the people of God.

In this chapter, I have only scratched the surface of the possibilities that exist. I pray to discover new ways to engage believers in discipleship in the coming months ahead. I pray the same for you, my friend. We need to be and grow disciples now more than ever.

EPILOGUE

> "Deep calls to deep
>   in the roar of your waterfalls;
> all your waves and breakers
>   have swept over me"
> *Psalm 42:7*

Discipleship is a deep calling.

A mysterious and beautiful work of God in each of our lives and in the lives of those we serve. It's a journey I'm committed to through the highs and lows.

I am grateful for this process.

Of loss and trust.

Pain and praise.

Tears and joy.

God, slowly bearing fruit in our lives.

I remain keenly aware of my smallness.

Yet, I grow increasingly aware of God's faithfulness.

In Ezekiel 37, God shows Ezekiel a vision. He sees a desperately dry valley, filled with bones. Lifeless and hopeless, it is in this place that God shows him the power of the Spirit to rejuvenate. Out of dry bones, God raises up a people of God. "You will know that I the Lord have spoken, and I have done it, declares the Lord" (Ezekiel 37:14).

God wanted Ezekiel to know, then, what God wants us to know now, "I have done it." "There is a work of bringing life through Spirit that you cannot do—only I can do," God says.

As I look in the valley, do I see lifeless bones or the children of God? As I look at the church, at people's lives, and at my own, do I look at the difficult and see possibility?

God is inviting us to see possibilities.

This book was written from my experience over the last decade, in lived ministry and shared life. The final process of putting words to page took place at a Christian retreat center, going between my kneeling in the prayer chapel, writing at a desk, and walking outside in the sanctuary of nature. I am praying for you and praying for me.

If you feel broken, remember "a bruised reed he will not break. A smoldering wick he will not snuff out" (Isaiah 42:3).

If you feel overwhelmed, remember the invitation of Jesus to "Come to me all you who are weary and burdened...learn from me" (Matthew 11:28-30).

If you feel hopeless, remember God promises to do "a new thing" in your midst (Isaiah 43:19).

Oh God,

Let us continue to learn this way, the way of discipleship.

Let us walk yoked with You.

May we respond to your deep calling in each of our lives.

May we live, knowing we are your beloved.

As we do, let us invite others to do the same.

In the name of our Master and Savior Jesus,

Amen.

ENDNOTES

CHAPTER ZERO

[1] Particularly Allan Walshe, Jan Johnson, Jon Dybdahl and S. Joseph Kidder.

[2] See the resource section for discipleship books, in addition to the research of Brené Brown.

[3] J. Dybdahl. *Hunger: Satisfying the Longing of Your Soul* (Hagerstown, MD: Autumn House, 2008).

[4] See "Deep Calling Curriculum" for all details regarding retreats and weekly meetings.

[5] B. Hull, *The Complete Book of Discipleship: On Being and Making Followers of Christ* (Colorado Springs, CO: NavPress, 2006), 228.

[6] I am grateful for phone interviews with Dr. Deborah Watson, Dr. A. Allan Martin, Dr. Matthew Gamble, and Dr. Sabine Vatel.

[7] G. Ogden. *Discipleship Essentials a Guide to Building Your Life in Christ* (Downers Grove, IL: IVP Connect, 2007).

[8] A. Stanley and B. Willits, *Creating Community* (Sisters, OR: Multnomah, 2004).

[9] Hull. *Discipleship*, 228.

CHAPTER ONE

[1] Eugene H. Peterson, *Eat This Book: A Conversation in the Art of Spiritual Reading* (Grand Rapids, MI: Eerdmans, 2009).

CHAPTER TWO

[1] Eugene H. Peterson, *A Long Obedience in the Same Direction: Discipleship in an Instant Society* (Downers Grove, IL: IVP Books, 2019).

CHAPTER THREE

[1] Ray Vander Laan, *In the Dust of the Rabbi: Small Group Edition Discovery Guide: Becoming a Disciple* (Grand Rapids, MI, 2006).

[2] W. A. Elwell, *Evangelical Dictionary of Biblical Theology* (Grand Rapids, MI: Baker Books, 1996).

³ A. W. Tozer, *The Pursuit of God* (Harrisburg, PA: First Christian Publications, 1982), 32.

⁴ E. G. H. White, *Our Father Cares: Devotional Readings for 1992* (Hagerstown, MD: Review and Herald, 1991), 40.

⁵ A. W. Tozer, *Keys to the Deeper Life* (Grand Rapids, MI: Zondervan, 1984), 30-31.

CHAPTER FOUR

¹ Erika Eichelberger, "Violence on the Home Front," Mother Jones, April 25, 2013, http://www.motherjones.com/politics/2013/04/domestic-violence-murder-stats/.

² Ellen G. White, *Counsels to Writers and Editors* (Nashville, TN: Southern, 1946), 33.

CHAPTER FIVE

¹ E. G. White, *Testimonies to Ministers and Gospel Workers* (Mountain View, CA: Pacific Press, 1923), 127.

² D. Bonhoeffer, *Life together: The Classic Exploration of Christian Community* (New York: HarperCollins, 1978).

³ Ibid.

⁴ E. G. White, "The Sign of Discipleship," *The Review and Herald,* July 21, 1903, para. 2.

CHAPTER SIX

¹ Dallas Willard, *Hearing God: Developing a Conversational Relationship with God* (Grand Rapids, MI: InterVarsity Press, 2005).

² Special thanks to Emily P. Freeman for featuring this on her podcast, *The Next Right Thing.*

³ Jon L. Dybdahl, *Hunger: Satisfying the Longing of Your Soul.* Hagerstown, MD: Autumn House, 2008), 13.

⁴ Russell Burrill, *Recovering an Adventist Approach to the Life and Mission of the Local Church* (Fallbrook, CA: Hart Research Center, 1998), 234.

⁵ With gratitude to Eugene Peterson for how he describes this.

⁶ Ellen White, *Special Testimonies on Education* (1897; repr. Silver Spring, MD: Ellen G. White Estate, 2017), 163.

CHAPTER SEVEN

1. Dan Jackson, Diversity Celebration Sermon, Silver Spring, MD, November 2012.

2. General Conference Ministerial Department, *Seventh-day Adventists Believe* (Silver Spring, MD: General Conference of Seventh-day Adventists, 2005).

3. Jay E. Adams, *Keeping the Sabbath Today?* (Stanley, NC: Timeless Texts; 2008); M. Finley, *When God said Remember* (Nampa, ID: Pacific Press, 2009).

4. R. R. Barton, *Sacred Rhythms: Arranging Our Lives for Spiritual Transformation* (Downers Grove, IL: InterVarsity Press, 2006); Jefferson Bethke, *To Hell with the Hustle: Reclaiming Your Life in an Overworked, Overspent, and Overconnected World* (Nashville, TN: Nelson, 2019); John Mark Comer and John Ortberg, *The Ruthless Elimination of Hurry: How to Stay Emotionally Healthy and Spiritually Alive in the Chaos of the Modern World* (New York: WaterBrook, 2019); P. Scazzero, *Emotionally Healthy Spirituality: Unleash a Revolution in Your Life in Christ* (Nashville, TN: Nelson, 2006); A. Swoboda, *Subversive Sabbath* (Ada, MI: Brazos Press, 2018).

5. J. Paulsen, *When the Spirit Descends* (Hagerstown, MD: Review and Herald, 2001), 113.

6. S. J. Kidder, *The Big Four: Secrets to a Thriving Church Family* (Hagerstown, MD: Review and Herald, 2011); Richard Rice, *The Reign of God: An Introduction to Christian Theology from a Seventh-day Adventist Perspective,* 2 Sub ed. (Berrien Springs, MI: Andrews University Press, 1997).

7. R. Burrill, *Recovering an Adventist Approach to the Life and Mission of the Local Church* (Fallbrook, CA: Hart Research Center, 1998), 17.

8. Allan Walshe, "Discipleship" (class lecture, Andrews University, 2011).

9. A. A. Martin, S. Bailey, and L. LaMountain, *God Encounters: Pursuing a 24/7 Experience of Jesus* (Nampa, ID: Pacific Press, 2009), 5.

10. M.Sahlin, *Adventist Congregations Today: New Evidence for Equipping Healthy Churches* (Lincoln, NE: Center for Creative Ministry, 2003); V. B. Gillespie and M. J. Donahue, *Valuegenesis: Ten Years Later: A Study of Two Generations* (Riverside, CA: Hancock Center, 2004); M. Tetz and G. L. Hopkins, *We Can Keep Them in the Church: How to Love Our Children So They Won't Leave* (Nampa, ID: Pacific Press, 2004).

11. Burrill, *Adventist Approach.*

12. See Acts 1 and 2; Ellen G. White, *The Acts of the Apostles* (Mountain View, CA: Pacific Press, 1911).

13. Paul X. Rutz, "The South Vietnam Pilot Who Performed a Daring Feat To Save His Family," *Historynet*, June 2019, https://www.historynet.com/maj-buang-lys-daring-feat-to-save-his-family.htm.

14. Ellen G. White, *Life Sketches of Ellen G. White* (1915; Mountain View, CA: Pacific Press , 1943), 196.

CHAPTER EIGHT

[1] G. Lyons, *The Next Christians: The Good News about the End of Christian America* (New York: Doubleday Religion, 2010), 192.

[2] R. McNeal, *A Work of Heart: Understanding How God Shapes Spiritual Leaders*, 1st ed. (San Francisco, CA: Jossey-Bass, 2000); D. Willard, *Hearing God: Developing a Conversational Relationship with God* (Grand Rapids, MI: InterVarsity Press, 2005).

[3] A book by this title, *Streams in the Desert* by L. B. Cowman, has been a great blessing to me. I recommend it!

CHAPTER NINE

[1] Ellen White, *Steps to Christ* (1892; Mountain View, CA: Pacific Press, 1956), 21.

[2] S. J. Kidder, *The Big Four: Secrets to a Thriving Church Family* (Hagerstown, MD: Review and Herald, 2011), 67.

[3] J. Dybdahl, *Hunger: Satisfying the Longing of Your Soul* (Hagerstown, MD: Autumn House, 2008), 13.

[4] A. A. Martin, S. Bailey, and L. LaMountain, *God Encounters: Pursuing a 24/7 Experience of Jesus* (Nampa, ID: Pacific Press, 2009), 7.

[5] D. Willard, *Hearing God: Developing a Conversational Relationship with God* (Grand Rapids, MI: InterVarsity Press, 2005).

[6] D. Bonhoeffer, *The Cost of Discipleship* (New York: Touchstone, 1995), 174.

[7] Jen Pollock Michel, *Surprised by Paradox: The Promise of "And" in an Either-Or World* (Downers Grove, IL: IVP Books, 2019).

[8] J. P. Moreland, *Kingdom Triangle: Recover the Christian Mind, Renovate the Soul, Restore the Spirit's Power* (Grand Rapids, MI: Zondervan, 2007).

[9] See Barton, 2006; Dybdahl, 2008; Foster, 2001; Kidder, 2011; Moreland, 2007; Mulholland, 1993.

[10] R. J. Foster, *Celebration of discipline: The Path to Spiritual Growth* (San Francisco, CA: HarperSanFrancisco, 1998).

[11] Moreland, *Kingdom Triangle*, 153.

[12] Lauren F. Winner, *Mudhouse Sabbath*. (Brewster, MA: Paraclete Press, 2003).

[13] Ellen G. White, *Faith and Works* (Nashville, TN: Southern, 1979), 48-49.

[14] Kidder, 75.

[15] D. G. Benner, *Sacred Companions: The Gift of Spiritual Friendship and Direction* (Downers Grove, IL: InterVarsity Press, 2002).

[16] R. R. Barton, *Sacred rhythms: Arranging Our Lives for Spiritual Transformation*

(Downers Grove, IL: InterVarsity Press, 2006).

[17] B. Hull, *The Complete Book of Discipleship: On Being and Making Followers of Christ* (Colorado Springs, CO: NavPress, 2006).

[18] White, Steps to Christ, 57.

[19] White, Steps to Christ, 63.

[20] Hull, *Book of Discipleship*, 24.

CHAPTER TEN

[1] R. R. Barton, *Sacred rhythms: Arranging Our Lives for Spiritual Transformation* (Downers Grove, IL: InterVarsity Press, 2006).

[2] P. Scazzero, *Emotionally Healthy Spirituality: Unleash a Revolution in Your Life in Christ*. (Nashville, TN: Nelson, 2006), 196.

[3] Ellen G. White, *Steps to Christ* (1892; Mountain View, CA: Pacific Press, 1956), 68.

[4] Ibid., 69.

[5] Ibid.

[6] Special thanks to Dr. Allan Walshe

[7] I am grateful to my friend and mentor Allan Walshe for the wording of these questions.

[8] Harvey Cox, *Feast of Fools* (Cambridge, MA: Harvard University Press, 1969), 12.

[9] White, *Steps to Christ*, 117.

[10] Henri J.M. Nouwen, *Here and Now* (New York: Crossroad, 1994).

[11] Eugene Peterson, *A Long Obedience in the Same Direction*, (Downers Grove, IL: IVP Books, 2019), 96.

CHAPTER ELEVEN

[1] Ellen G. White, *Steps to Christ* (Mountain View, CA: Pacific Press, 1956), 93.

[2] Charles H. Spurgeon, *Morning and Evening: A New Edition of the Classic Devotional Based on the Holy Bible, English Standard Version*, rev., updated ed. (Wheaton, IL: Crossway, 2003).

[3] M. Robert Mulholland Jr., *Invitation to a Journey: A Road Map for Spiritual Formation* (Downers Grove, IL: IVP Books, 2016).

[4] Henri J. M. Nouwen, *Reaching Out: The Three Movements of the Spiritual Life*, reissue ed. (New York: Image, Doubleday, 1986).

[5] J. Dybdahl, *Hunger: Satisfying the Longing of Your Soul* (Hagerstown, MD: Autumn House, 2008).

[6] Paul E. Miller and David Powlison, *A Praying Life: Connecting with God in a Distracting World*, rev. ed. (Colorado Springs, CO: NavPress, 2017).

[7] These are two apps I use regularly in ministry and in my devotional practice.

[8] Ellen G. White, *The Ministry of Healing* (1905; Mountain View, CA: Pacific Press, 1942), 58.

[9] Ellen G. White, *Christ's Object Lessons* (1900; Washington, DC: Review and Herald, 1941), 174.

[10] Dallas Willard, *In Search of Guidance* (Ventura, CA: Regal Books, 1984), 214.

CHAPTER TWELVE

[1] Orlando Sentinel, "Unplanned Ride: Tattoo the Basset Hound Went..." *Orlando Sentinel*, March 10, 1990, https://www.orlandosentinel.com/news/os-xpm-1990-03-10-9003103334-story.html.

[2] J. H. Walton, *Genesis: The NIV Application Commentary* (Grands Rapids, MI: Zondervan Academic, 2011).

[3] Judith Shulemitz, "Bring Back the Sabbath," *New York Times*, March 2, 2003, https://www.nytimes.com/2003/03/02/magazine/bring-back-the-sabbath.html.

[4] *NET Bible, Full Notes Edition* (Nashville, TN: Nelson, 1996).

[5] Jan. Johnson, *When the Soul Listens: Finding Rest and Direction in Contemplative Prayer* (Colorado Springs, CO: NavPress, 2017).

[6] Dallas Willard, *The Spirit of the Disciplines: Understanding How God Changes Lives*, repr. ed. (New York: HarperCollins, 1990), 180.

CHAPTER THIRTEEN

[1] C. L. Lyons, "Loneliness and Social Isolation," *CQ Researcher* 28 (August 3, 2018): 657-680, http://library.cqpress.com/.

[2] Tim Adams, "John Cacioppo: 'Loneliness Is Like an Iceberg–It Goes Deeper than We Can See,'" *The Guardian*, February 28, 2016, https://www.theguardian.com/science/2016/feb/28/loneliness-is-like-an-iceberg-john-cacioppo-social-neuroscience-interview.

[3] D. Ramsey, *EntreLeadership: 20 Years of Practical Business Wisdom from the Trenches* (New York: Howard Books, 2011), 231.

[4] A. Stanley and B. Willits, *Creating Community* (Sisters, OR: Multnomah, 2004), 22.

[5] K. Meyer, "The Megachurch and the Monastery," *Leadership Journal* 30, no. 1 (Winter 2009), http://www.christianitytoday.com/le/2009/winter/megachurchmonastery.html.

[6] H. Cloud and J. S. Townsend, *Making Small Groups Work: What Every Small Group Leader Needs to Know* (Grand Rapids, MI: Zondervan, 2003).

[7] A. A. Martin, S. Bailey, and L. LaMountain, *God Encounters: Pursuing a 24/7 Experience of Jesus* (Nampa, ID: Pacific Press, 2009).

[8] Stanley and Willits, *Creating Community*, 12.

[9] Cloud and Townsend, *Small Groups*, 82.

[10] Cloud and Townsend, *Small Groups*, 82.

[11] D. Bonhoeffer, *Life Together: The Classic Exploration of Christian Community* (New York: HarperCollins, 1939).

[12] E. G. White, "The Sign of Discipleship," *The Review and Herald*, July 21, 1903, para. 2.

[13] Helen Murphy, "Eight Spellers Just Won the 2019 National Spelling Bee in an Unprecedented Tie," *People*, May 31, 2019, https://people.com/human-interest/eight-spellers-win-national-spelling-bee-2019-tie/.

[14] Jean Carnahan, *Don't Let the Fire Go Out* (Columbia, MI: University of Missouri Press, 2004).

CHAPTER FOURTEEN

[1] Kathleen Norris, *Acedia & Me: A Marriage, Monks, and a Writer's Life*, repr. ed. (New York: Riverhead Books, 2010), 190.

[2] D. G. Benner, *Sacred Companions: The Gift of Spiritual Friendship and Direction* (Downers Grove, IL: InterVarsity Press, 2002), 35.

[3] H. Cloud and J. S. Townsend, *Boundaries: When to Say Yes, When to Say No to Take Control of Your Life* (Grand Rapids, MI: Zondervan, 1992).

[4] D. A. Seamands, *Healing for Damaged Emotions* (Wheaton, IL: Victor Books, 1981).

[5] R. McNeal, *A Work of Heart: Understanding How God Shapes Spiritual Leaders* (San Francisco: Jossey-Bass, 2000); R. A. Swenson, *Margin: Restoring Emotional, Physical, Financial, and Time Reserves to Overloaded Lives* (Colorado Springs, CO: NavPress, 2004).

[6] P. Scazzero, *Emotionally Healthy Spirituality: Unleash a Revolution in Your Life in Christ* (Nashville, TN: Nelson, 2006), 12.

[7] Jon Dybdahl, "Theological and Historical Perspectives on Spiritual Growth" (class lecture, Orlando, FL, February 15, 2010).

[8] R. Burrill, *Recovering an Adventist Approach to the Life and Mission of the Local Church* (Fallbrook, CA: Hart Research Center, 1998), 18.

[9] D. Bonhoeffer, *The Cost of Discipleship* (New York: Touchstone, 1959).

[10] Scazzero, *Emotionally Healthy Spirituality*, 138.

[11] Ibid., 140.

[12] Ibid., 152.

[13] Bonhoeffer, *Cost of Discipleship*, 104.

[14] B. Hull, *The Complete Book of Discipleship: On Being and Making Followers of Christ* (Colorado Springs, CO: NavPress, 2006).

[15] J. Cymbala and D. Merrill, *Fresh Wind, Fresh Fire: What Happens When God's Spirit Invades the Heart of His People* (Grand Rapids, MI: Zondervan, 1997), 57-58.

[16] R. McNeal, *A Work of Heart: Understanding How God Shapes Spiritual Leaders* (San Fransisco: Jossey-Bass, 2000).

[17] "Tikkun olam," *Wikipedia*, last updated February 14, 2020, https://en.wikipedia.org/wiki/Tikkun_olam.

[18] Leontine Kelly, "We Need Healing," Day 1, May 03, 1998, https://day1.org/weekly-broadcast/5d9b820ef71918cdf200255d/we_need_healing.

[19] Ibid.

CHAPTER FIFTEEN

[1] A. Lindgren and T. Ross, *Pippi Goes Aboard* (Oxford, UK: Oxford University Press, 2002), 10-11.

[2] Malcolm Goldsmith, *Knowing Me, Knowing God: Exploring Your Spirituality with Myers-Briggs* (Nashville, TN: Abingdon Press, 1997), 6.

[3] D. R. Dick and B. Miller, *Equipped for Every Good Work: Building a Gifts-Based Church* (Eugene, OR: Wipf & Stock, 2011).

[4] H. Kuhalampi, "Holistic Spirituality as a Key to Understanding Ellen White," *Spectrum Magazine*, January 10, 2011, 1.

[5] J. P. Moreland, *Kingdom Triangle: Recover the Christian Mind, Renovate the Soul, Restore the Spirit's Power* (Grand Rapids, MI: Zondervan, 2007), 146.

[6] B. Hull, *The Complete Book of Discipleship: On Being and Making Followers of Christ* (Colorado Springs, CO: NavPress, 2006).

[7] R. Warren, *The Purpose Driven Life: What on Earth Am I Here For?* (Grand Rapids, MI: Zondervan, 2002).

[8] S. Godin, *Lynchpin: Are You Indispensable?* (New York: Penguin, 2010), 25.

[9] Warren, *The Purpose Driven Life*, 17.

[10] D. Willard, *Hearing God: Developing a Conversational Relationship with God* (Grand Rapids, MI: InterVarsity Press, 2005).

[11] R. Stearns, *The Hole in Our Gospel: What does God Expect of Us? The Answer that Changed My Life and Might Just Change the World* (Nashville, TN: Nelson, 2009), 123.

[12] J. Paulsen, *When the Spirit Descends* (Hagerstown, MD: Review and Herald, 2001), 79.

[13] R. Stearns, *The Hole in Our Gospel*, 59.

[14] R. J. Foster, *Celebration of Discipline: The Path to Spiritual Growth* (San Francisco: HarperSanFrancisco, 1998), 137, 187.

[15] K. Humphreys and D. Humphreys, *Show and Then Tell: Presenting the Gospel through Daily Encounters* (Chicago: Moody Press, 2000), 25.

[16] B. D. McLaren, *More Ready Than You Realize: The Power of Everyday Conversations* (Grand Rapids, MI: Zondervan, 2002), 41.

[17] R. Burrill, *Recovering an Adventist Approach to the Life and Mission of the Local Church* (Fallbrook, CA: Hart Research Center, 1998), 23.

[18] F. Chan and M. Beuving, *Multiply: Disciples Making Disciples* (Colorado Springs, CO: Cook, 2012).

CHAPTER SIXTEEN

[1] R. Stearns, *The Hole in Our Gospel* (Nashville, TN: Nelson, 2009), 59.

[2] S. Claiborne, *The Irresistible Revolution* (Grand Rapids, MI: Zondervan, 2006), 296.

[3] Stearns, *The Hole in Our Gospel*, 24.

[4] Ellen White, *Steps to Christ* (1892; Mountain View, CA: Pacific Press, 1956), 68.

[5] S. Miles. *Take This Bread: A Radical Conversion* (New York: Ballantine Books, 2007), xvi.

[6] L. Y. Abramson, M. E. Seligman, and J. D. Teasdale. "Learned Helplessness in Humans: Critique and Reformulation," *Journal of Abnormal Psychology* 87, no. 1: (1978), 49–74.

[7] Dale Carnegie, quoted in Joseph O'Day, *The Ring of Truth: Truth and Wisdom in J. R. R. Tolkien's The Lord of the Rings* (Maitland, FL: Xulon Press, 2004).

[8] Dallard Willard. (1935-2013) American philosopher and philosophy professor who wrote books on Christianity and Christian Living.

[9] Eugene H. Peterson, *Eat This Book: A Conversation in the Art of Spiritual Reading* (Grand Rapids, MI: Eerdmans, 2009).

[10] Brad Limerick (Catalyst Conference. Orange County, CA, April 2019).

[11] Janet Weinstein, "Hit by Harvey, Young People in Rockport, Texas, Open Impromptu Shelter," *ABC News*, August 27, 2017, https://abcnews.go.com/US/harvey-young-people-open-impromptu-shelter-rockport-texas/story?id=49451898.

[12] Clara Booth Luce. (1903-1987) American author, playwright, journalist, and the first American woman appointed to a major ambassadorial post abroad.

CHAPTER SEVENTEEN

[1] John Trent, Gary Smalley, and Kari Trent Stageberg, *The Blessing: Giving the Gift of Unconditional Love and Acceptance*, rev., exp. ed. (Nashville, TN: Nelson, 2019).

[2] The Posse Foundation, 2020, https://www.possefoundation.org.

[3] Henri Nouwen, *Life of the Beloved*, quoted in Cathlynn Law, "Beloved of God" (sermon, United Church in University Place, January 13, 2019), http://ucup.org/multimedia-archive/beloved-of-god/.

CHAPTER EIGHTEEN

[1] E. G. White, *Steps to Christ* (1892; Mountain View, CA: Pacific Press, 1956), 69.

[2] E. G. White, *Counsels to Writers and Editors* (Nashville, TN: Southern, 1946), 35.

[3] S. J. Kidder, *The Big Four: Secrets to a Thriving Church Family* (Hagerstown, MD: Review and Herald, 2011), 75.

[4] B. Hull, *The Complete Book of Discipleship: On Being and Making Followers of Christ* (Colorado Springs, CO: NavPress, 2006), 238.

[5] Wendy Walshe, class lecture, Discipleship, Berrien Springs, MI, 2011.

[6] Bill Hull, *Complete Book of Discipleship*, 233.

CHAPTER TWENTY

[1] Jules Renard, *The Journal of Jules Renard* (March, 1906), ed. and trans. Louise Bogan and Elizabeth Roget (Portland, OR: Tin House Books, 2008), 234.

[2] B. Hull, *The Complete Book of Discipleship: On Being and Making Followers of Christ* (Colorado Springs, CO: NavPress, 2006).

[3] I'm grateful for Chan (2012) and Ogden (2007) who shared their process.

[4] G. Barna, *Growing True Disciples: New Strategies for Producing Genuine Followers of Christ* (Colorado Springs, CO: WaterBrook Press, 2001), 162.

[5] Henry Newbolt, "The Building of the Temple," in *Poems: Old and New* (n.p., Hotfree Books, n.d.), http://www.hotfreebooks.com/book/Poems-New-and-Old-Henry-Newbolt--2.html.

[6] James Clear, *Atomic Habits: An Easy and Proven Way to Build Good Habits and Break Bad Ones* (New York: Avery, 2018).

CHAPTER TWENTY-ONE

[1] Special thanks to Pastor Nick Snell for modeling creative ways to connect during this Pandemic.

[2] Special thanks to Pastor Jessie López, Stephanie and Lydia Zebedeus who showed us how fun this idea could be!

APPENDIX

Personal Assessment

Call to Devotion

Call to Healing

Call to Community

Call to Serve

Call to Witness

Where do you stand with God?

Talk about three major areas of brokenness that you are experiencing in your life.

Talk about three areas of joy that you are experiencing in your life.

Briefly describe your current devotional life.

Discover your Myers-Briggs Personality Type by taking the inventory online.

One site that offers this for free is: http://www.humanmetrics.com/cgi-win/jtypes2.asp

Discover your Love Language by taking the inventory at:

http://www.5lovelanguages.com/profile/

Discover your Spiritual Gifts by taking the inventory at:

http://www.spiritualgiftstest.com/test/adult

JOIN THE MOVEMENT

Go to **taravincross.com/deepcalling/** to download FREE videos, devotional resources, and new group activities.

Sign up to be a facilitator and unlock access to promotional videos and materials for launching your own discipleship group.

DEEP CALLING
DISCIPLESHIP RESOURCES

Book • Curriculum • Participant Journal

AdventSource
www.adventsource.org

DEEP CALLING will support your church leadership team as you work to establish an effective discipleship process.

Quantity discounts available